Antony Worrall Thompson

The Essential
Low Fat Cookbook

Good healthy eating for every day

with an introduction by
Juliette Kellow BSc RD

In association with **HEART UK** –
The Cholesterol Charity

Photography by Georgia Glynn Smith

Kyle Books

First published in Great Britain in 2011 by
Kyle Books
23 Howland Street, London W1T 4AY
general.enquiries@kylebooks.com
www.kylebooks.com

10 9 8 7 6 5 4 3 2 1

ISBN 978-1-85626-977-3

Project editor: Judith Hannam
Photographer: Georgia Glynn Smith
Food stylist: Aya Nishimura
Props stylist: Nadine Tubbs
Designer: Jacqui Caulton
Editorial assistants: Elanor Clarke and Laura Foster
Production: Gemma John
Copy editor: Emily Hatchwell
Proof reader: Clare Hubbard
Indexer: Helen Snaith

A Cataloguing In Publication record for this
title is available from the British Library.

Printed and bound by 1010 Printing International Ltd.

Dedication

To Paul Mullen

who needs to eat

more food like this...

he knows it,

and he's a great cook.

Contents

Foreword by HEART UK
The Cholesterol Charity

It is refreshing to see *The Essential Low Fat Cookbook* in print, proving that indulgent food can be appetising and enjoyable even if it is not loaded with fat, salt and sugar. Juliette Kellow provides a wonderful introduction to this book detailing the reasons why we should all limit our fat intake.

Eating healthily is not only about watching your total fat intake, it's also about the quality and balance of fats in your diet. As a first step, cutting back on saturated fat is the best way to limit total fat intake. For positive heart health, and whenever you use fats in cooking, health professionals recommend you use seed, nut and vegetable oils as these provide vital mono and polyunsaturated fatty acids. As Juliette points out on page 26, you should still limit the amount of these oils that you use in your cooking because they are concentrated sources of both fat and calories. Not only do Antony Worrall Thompson's magnificent recipes make it easy for the cook by setting out the right balance between saturated fats and unsaturated fats, but each recipe details its nutritional composition. For those concerned about keeping their cholesterol levels low this book is a valuable asset.

Not all high fat foods should be avoided equally, oily fish has a special place in the diet and is universally recommended once a week, and following a heart attack health professionals advise eating 2–4 portions of oily fish every week or a supplement containing 1g daily of the omega 3 oils, DHA and EPA for up to 4 years.

Whilst nuts are considered high in fats, what many people do not know is that they are also cardio-protective. This is because of the range of nutrients that they provide, including the heart-healthy mono-unsaturated fatty acids, naturally occurring plant sterols, vegetable fibre, vitamins E, magnesium, potassium and other plant substances. So whilst it is important to avoid an excessive intake of nuts, they can still be incorporated into recipes and used as snacks as part of a low fat approach to eating.

At HEART UK we are passionate about preventing premature deaths caused by high cholesterol and cardiovascular disease. We also work to raise awareness about the risks of high cholesterol, lobby for better detection of those at risk and support health professional training. It's also why we work with a variety of partners to promote healthier lifestyle options.

We are always delighted to hear from people with raised cholesterol and their families and we can provide advice and support via our helpline (0845 450 5988). One of the things we get asked for most are ideas for healthy meals and snacks to help lower cholesterol. Having picked up this book we hope you share our enthusiasm for it and we hope you get pleasure from making and sharing these recipes with friends.

Jules Payne
Chief Executive
HEART UK – The Cholesterol Charity

From AWT

For me to write a low-fat cookbook is a bit like having only two peas in a pod, as fat is important to chefs. We tell everyone that fat is where the flavour comes from; we love butter, cream, pork fat, beef fat, dripping, crackling, chicken skin and streaky bacon – don't tell me you don't too! Unfortunately, flavoursome as these fats all are, they have a nasty habit of clogging up your pipes and contain a high amount of calories which don't flatter the waistband.

So why am I writing a low-fat cookbook? Well, to be honest, I'm in the healthy groove, having written five books geared towards people with diabetes, I love to prove that you can diet and still enjoy your food. I'm not a health messiah, but I do intend over the next few years to tackle many of the problem eating areas that plague us all. I enjoy being challenged; how do you cook lovely food when you can't use the chefs' favourite ingredient, fat?

So I've done my world tour, looked at all the dishes I enjoy eating, and then analysed them to see if they can enter the low-fat zone. Some dishes couldn't and hit the cutting-room floor, but many could as, with the addition of one or two spices or herbs, you can more than compensate for the flavour lost through omitting fat.

I have to be honest, I don't necessarily think the establishment has got it all right in the omission of all fats – there are good fats and there are bad fats – but I've been a good lad and done just that. But I still hanker after the day the medical experts tell us that we don't have to cut back too stringently on that avocado, olive and rapeseed oil, and that it's okay to eat high-fat fish as we know they are very good for the heart.

But I'm sure you're not interested in my fantasies! You've been told by your doc that all fat must go and that's the reason you're thumbing through this book. But it's *you* who has to decide what food style suits you best; you must work out an eating plan that you can achieve, and by using the recipes in this book I hope you'll realise that even if you've been put on a strict regime by your doctor you can still look forward to each meal.

I've read the books, seen the movie and worn the T-shirt, and so many recipes that stick to the rules can only be described as disappointing. Let me try and change all that by giving you a diverse collection of low-fat recipes from around the world. You'll recognise many of the recipe names — cooking isn't rocket science after all, it's a rubber ball that comes bouncing back to home; it's been done before but I hope I've added that little *je ne sais quoi* which makes my dishes jump off the pages of this book and into your psyche.

I've had fun writing this book, my pen has flowed with enjoyment and I'll tell you something, I feel better for it and I've lost loads of weight as a side effect, so that can't be bad.

Now back to that treadmill . . .

Antony Worrall Thompson

Low-fat low-down

by Juliette Kellow BSc RD

Think of a low-fat diet and, for many of us, that instantly conjures up images of bland, boring food that we derive little pleasure from eating. It's a diet we choose simply because it's 'good for us', when in reality we'd much rather be munching our way through a mouth-watering plate of creamy pasta or a juicy pan-fried steak.

Well, congratulations on picking up this book! Whether you want to lose weight, look after your heart, eat more healthily or follow a low-fat diet to help you with a specific health problem, we guarantee that *The Essential Low Fat Cookbook* is for you. It's packed with delicious recipes that you'll actually want to cook and eat. Better still, your taste buds won't even realise that what you're eating is low in fat.

We've provided detailed nutrition information per serving for every single recipe in this book, including calories, fat, saturates, sugars, salt and fibre. Plus we've provided the nutrition information for fat per 100g. We've followed in the footsteps of food companies and decided to use the same definition of 'low-fat' as supermarkets and manufacturers. That helps to make it less confusing for you — and means that every recipe in this book contains 3g fat or less per 100g.

Eating a diet that contains too much saturated fat is a real problem in the Western world, which is sadly reflected in a range of associated health problems including heart disease and obesity, two major diseases that are well established as causing premature death. It's no surprise that health professionals recommend cutting back on the amount of fat we consume.

But eating the low-fat way isn't just great for shifting excess pounds and helping to keep the heart healthy. A low-fat diet can also help to reduce the risk of insulin resistance, a condition that's often a warning sign for Type 2 diabetes. Meanwhile, low-fat diets can be used as part of a treatment programme for a variety of health conditions such as gallstones or gall bladder disease.

Many of us struggle to stick to a low-fat way of eating though, usually because we get bored of the same old low-fat ingredients day in, day out. Bizarrely, some of us even go as far as choosing foods we don't like that much, making mealtimes even more of a penance than a pleasure. And then, we have a tendency to be unimaginative when it comes to preparing these ingredients. It's no surprise that a diet consisting of little other than grilled chicken or fish, salads and jacket potatoes with cottage cheese quickly turns off our taste buds and leaves us craving a huge plate of fish and chips or chicken korma with pilau rice.

That's where *The Essential Low Fat Cookbook* comes to the rescue. Sure, fat adds flavour to food, but armed with a few tips and tricks — and a handful of staple, flavoursome ingredients in your kitchen — it's easy to turn even the plainest chicken breast or piece of cod into a culinary delight, without drowning it in oil, butter or cream. Better still, you don't need to give up red meat, cheese and eggs — or even puddings and cakes for that matter. As you turn the pages, chances are you'll be delighted to find that many of your long-held beliefs about low-fat diets are actually nothing more than myths.

Why a low-fat diet?

Scientific studies show that having too much fat, particularly saturated fat, in our diets is associated with a long list of health problems. The good news is that health experts agree that cutting down on fat by following a low-fat diet can help to reduce our risk of many of these conditions.

Keep your heart healthy

Without doubt, cardiovascular disease (CVD) – which includes all the diseases of the heart and circulatory system – is the one condition everyone links to diets high in saturated fat. With good reason. According to the World Health Organization, in 2005 no less than 17.5 million people died of the condition, accounting for 30 per cent of all deaths throughout the world.

In the UK, statistics from the British Heart Foundation reveal that CVD is the number one killer, responsible for a staggering 35 per cent of all deaths. About half of these are from coronary heart disease (which includes heart attacks and angina) and another quarter from strokes. It's an even grimmer picture for other European countries. Data from European Cardiovascular Disease Statistics shows that CVD causes 38 per cent of deaths in Norway, 40 per cent in Germany and a staggering 48 per cent in Greece, despite the commonly held belief that a Mediterranean diet is good for the heart. Even France, which is often highlighted as having much lower rates of CVD, sees 29 per cent of its population dying from the condition. In total, 48 per cent of deaths in Europe are caused by the condition.

It's a similar picture throughout the Western world. In Canada, 32 per cent of people die from CVD. In America, the incidence stands at 37 per cent. Meanwhile, on the other side of the world, just over a third of Australians die from the condition while in New Zealand, it jumps to 40 per cent.

It's well established that many factors are linked to an increased risk of cardiovascular disease, including things that we can't change, such as being male, having a family history of the condition (especially where family members have a heart attack, angina or die from heart disease before the age of 55 in a man or 65 in a woman), being of South Asian origin and simply getting older. There are also many risk factors that we can alter such as not smoking and being more active. That's where changing our eating habits comes into play. It's widely accepted that diets high in fat, particularly saturated fat – the type found predominantly in foods such as butter, lard, hard margarines, ghee, full-fat dairy products and meat – have a part to play in the development of CVD.

In particular, high intakes of fat (especially saturates) increase blood cholesterol, which is one of the major risk factors for coronary heart disease. It's something most of us need to worry about, too, even if we're female – it's a total myth that only men suffer with high cholesterol. Figures from the British Heart Foundation reveal that 57 per cent of men and 61 per cent of women in England have high cholesterol. The solution: cut down on fat to reduce your risk of high cholesterol, which in turn eliminates one of the risk factors for the number one killer disease. And over the course of this book, we'll show you just how to do that.

Stay slim

Unless you've been living on Mars for the last decade, it probably comes as no surprise to learn that obesity is a major health problem in the Western world. According to the World Health Organization (WHO), currently more than 1 billion adults around the world are overweight, and at least 300 million of them are clinically obese.

In the UK, 61 per cent of adults have a weight problem, while in America it's 67 per cent and in Canada 59 per cent. Within Europe, Italy has one of the lowest incidences of weight problems, although 44 per cent of the population are still classified as overweight or obese. This rises to 49 per cent in France, 57 per cent in Greece and 67 per cent in Germany. The picture is just as bad in the Southern Hemisphere, where 49 per cent of Australians,

63 per cent of New Zealanders and 45 per cent of South Africans are too heavy. Meanwhile, even those countries with no tradition of weight problems are now seeing the incidence rise: 19 per cent of Chinese, 23 per cent of Japanese, 32 per cent of Thais and 41 per cent of Brazilians are now overweight or obese. You get the picture: being fat is unfortunately all too common around the world.

Expanding waistlines come with an extensive list of health problems, including raised blood pressure and cholesterol, both of which are risk factors for CVD. Being overweight, even by a small amount, dramatically increases the risk of Type 2 diabetes, too – in fact, the World Health Organization believes that nine out of 10 people with the condition are overweight or obese. Then there's the increased risk of a range of cancers (see right). Overweight and obese adults are also more likely to suffer with gallstones, osteoarthritis, breathing difficulties, skin problems, infertility, sleep disturbances and mental health problems such as depression.

The question of whether it's simply fat that makes us fat has been debated by scientists for years. We know for sure that excessive weight gain occurs when our energy (or calorie) intake from food and drink exceeds the amount of energy (or calories) that we burn off. As a result, most experts agree that no one food, nutrient or group of foods makes us fat. It's our overall calorie intake that dictates whether we end up loosening or tightening our belts.

Nevertheless, fat can have a dramatic effect on that calorie content. Fat is a concentrated source of energy, providing nine kilocalories per gram – twice as many as the same amount of protein or carbohydrate. As a result, foods that contain a lot of fat also tend to be high in calories. And when we regularly take in too many calories, the pounds start to pile on.

Meanwhile, despite adding calories, fat adds very little actual quantity to our diet. This may be important as research shows that it's the actual quantity of food that we eat that helps to fill us up

and make us feel satisfied. For example, 200g of mashed potatoes contain 144 calories and 0.2g fat. Add 15g butter and that portion of mash (which now weighs just 15g more) provides 255 calories and 12.5g fat. The reality: we've added 8 per cent more food but a massive 44 per cent more calories.

Other research shows that fat seems to have a less satiating or filling effect than other food components such as protein and fibre, with the result that when we have a high-fat diet it's harder to satisfy hunger so we end up eating more. Then there's the effect that fat has on our taste buds. Undoubtedly, it helps to make food taste good – especially when it's combined with sugar, processed carbs or salt – so that we're more likely to overeat.

The reality: when we eat a high-fat diet, it's easy to consume a large number of calories – and if we don't burn these off, we risk becoming obese and suffering a range of health problems. So cutting down on fat (especially saturated fat) makes sense if we want to control our weight, or lose excess pounds.

Myth makeover

The myth: Low-fat and fat-free foods are low in calories.

The makeover: Foods that are described as 'low-fat' or 'fat-free' aren't automatically low in calories or calorie-free. In fact, some low-fat products may actually be higher in calories than standard products, thanks to them containing extra sugars and thickeners to boost the flavour and texture. Some people also mistakenly believe that they can eat more if they're choosing low-fat products. But this is rarely the case. In reality, two low-fat biscuits, for example, will probably contain more calories than one standard biscuit.

Protect yourself from cancer

An excess of body fat is one of the greatest risk factors for many cancers. According to the World Cancer Research Fund, excessive body fat increases the risk of cancers of the oesophagus, pancreas, bowel, endometrium, kidney and breast, and probably also puts us at risk for cancers of the gall bladder and liver.

The World Cancer Research Fund also reveals that high-fat diets themselves – regardless of weight – are linked to an increased risk of lung cancer, the most common type in the world, making up 13 per cent of all cancers. High-fat diets are also linked to breast cancer, the most common cancer in women, especially post-menopausal breast cancer. Meanwhile, foods containing animal fat may contribute to an increased risk of colorectal or bowel cancer, representing a tenth of all cancers globally. So cut down on fat and you also help to lower your chances of developing certain cancers.

Fight insulin resistance

Obesity is one of the major risk factors for insulin resistance. However, scientists are discovering increasingly that high fat intakes, particularly of saturated fats, are linked to insulin resistance, independently of body weight. In contrast, polyunsaturated fats and monounsaturated fats seem to improve insulin sensitivity.

The problem with insulin resistance is that it's a forerunner of Type 2 diabetes – a condition that's becoming increasingly common in Western countries. In this condition, the body's cells don't respond properly to the insulin produced by the pancreas; in other words, the cells are resistant to the effects of insulin, a hormone that regulates blood sugar levels. As a result, the pancreas continues to pump out more and more insulin to keep blood sugar levels within normal limits. Eventually the pancreas fails to keep up with this increased demand for insulin, so blood sugar levels rise and the stage is set for Type 2 diabetes.

The link between high fat intakes and insulin resistance is an area of science that needs more research, but inevitably it seems that cutting back on fat may help to lower the chances of insulin resistance and Type 2 diabetes.

Guard against gallstones

Being overweight increases the risk of gallstones – and the more overweight you are, the more the risk rises. According to the National Institute of Diabetes and Digestive and Kidney Disease, however, high-fat diets may also make a person more susceptible to them.

Gallstones are small stones that form in the gall bladder or its ducts. They occur when bile – which helps to digest fats – forms stones made from, among other things, hardened cholesterol-like material (this has nothing to do with cholesterol levels in the blood). Bile is made in the liver, then passes through a series of 'passageways' called bile ducts, into the gall bladder, where it is stored. The gall bladder then releases bile into the digestive system whenever it's needed to digest fat.

Although it's still an area that's being researched, it's thought that high-fat diets increase the risk of gallstones because the liver produces bile with a higher cholesterol content. The cholesterol begins to form small crystals, which then join together to form stones.

Gallstones often don't cause any symptoms, but if they get trapped in the bile ducts they can prevent the normal flow of bile, which results in sporadic abdominal pain. In severe cases, gallstones can trigger inflammation of the gall bladder, known as cholecystitis, resulting in symptoms such as a fever, constant stomach pains and even jaundice.

Health professionals agree that losing weight is one of the best things you can do to reduce the risk of developing gallstones, and ease symptoms if you already have them. But it's important to do this slowly, as rapid weight loss – more than two to three pounds per week – is actually associated with a greater risk of gallstones. This is because during crash diets, when body fat is broken down to supply energy, extra cholesterol is released into the bile. Indeed, people who follow very low-calorie diets or have weight-loss surgery are at high risk of gallstones.

Eating a low-fat diet can also help to ease the symptoms of gallstones (though the only way you can actually get rid of them is to have surgery). Unsurprisingly, pain caused by gallstones often comes after eating a fatty meal, when the gall bladder needs to release bile to digest the fat. Therefore, a lower-fat diet means that less bile is needed, so the gall bladder doesn't need to work as hard.

Get a better night's sleep

Believe it or not, a few studies show that high fat intakes, especially during the evening, may disrupt our sleep patterns. One small Brazilian study, for example, found that when volunteers had a high fat intake throughout the day, or just a high-fat dinner, they woke more frequently during the night as a result of tossing and turning, were more likely to suffer with abnormal breathing while sleeping, and spent less time in REM sleep – the type of sleep that helps to really rest and restore the body.

In another study from the University of Arizona, women who had high intakes of fat and saturates were far more likely to suffer with breathing disorders while they were sleeping, regardless of their weight. In fact, they consumed 28g more of fat a day than those women who didn't suffer with sleep disturbances. Whether it's sleep disturbance that results in a higher intake of fat the next day or a high-fat diet that causes poorer sleep, remains unclear. It's certainly an area that needs a lot more research before any definitive conclusions can be made. But if you have trouble sleeping, it certainly won't do any harm to cut down on fat and see if it makes a difference.

Breathe easy

It may not seem like an obvious link, but scientists are increasingly discovering that high-fat diets may aggravate the symptoms of asthma and may also make asthma medication less effective. In a recent Australian study, researchers discovered that asthma sufferers who ate a burger and chips containing 60g fat had lungs that were more inflamed than asthma sufferers who ate a low-fat yogurt containing just 3g fat. Treatment for asthma was also less effective in the burger eaters.

In another study, this time from Spain, increased intakes of saturated fats and particularly butter were linked to asthma in children. Yet more research from Kansas State University looked at the effect of a high-fat meal on lung function, and concluded that high-fat diets may contribute to chronic inflammatory diseases of the airway and lungs.

The link between fat intakes and breathing is another relatively new area of research and many more large-scale studies need to be carried out before any definite conclusions can be made. But early investigations certainly seem to link high-fat intakes with breathing difficulties.

Treat health problems

Diets that are low in saturated fat are recommended to treat a range of health problems, including to lower blood cholesterol or lose weight, or as part of the dietary treatment for insulin resistance, Type 2 diabetes and gallstones, frequently in combination with losing weight, if necessary.

Low-fat diets are usually also advised for people who have had surgery for weight loss such as gastric bands or bypasses, although it's important that anyone who's about to undergo or who has had such a procedure follows the specific advice of their consultant. Meanwhile, low-fat diets are often recommended to treat a range of other complaints, including some digestive disorders, but again the advice of a doctor or dietitian should always be followed.

Getting to grips with the guidelines

Advice on the maximum amount of fat we should eat varies from country to country. Generally speaking, in developed countries, it's based on preventing chronic diseases such as heart disease.

Most health agencies around the world express their recommendations for maximum fat intakes as a percentage of calories that should come from fat rather than an actual number of grams of fat. This may seem complicated, but it's done this way because not everyone has the same calorie needs – for example, men tend to need more calories than women because they are physically bigger. Using these percentage guidelines, health professionals can then work out suitable fat intakes for different groups of people – and provide advice on the maximum grams of fat they should aim for.

To prevent cardiovascular disease, most health agencies – including the Department of Health in the UK – recommend that no more than a third of our calories come from fat and no more than one tenth from saturates.

Some countries also recommend a lower limit to help ensure that populations don't have intakes that are so low they fail to get enough calories, healthy fats or fat-soluble vitamins. In America, for example, while the upper limit is set at 35 per cent of calories from fat and 10 per cent from saturates, the United States Department of Agriculture also recommends that no fewer than 20 per cent of calories come from fat. In Australia and New Zealand, the recommendations are the same.

On a global level, the World Health Organization recommends no fewer than 15 per cent of calories come from fat, although women of reproductive age and underweight adults should have no fewer than 20 per cent. At the other end of the scale, the WHO confirms that most people should get no more than 30–35 per cent of calories from fat.

But while there are clear guidelines as to the maximum amount of fat we should eat to prevent chronic diseases and the minimum amount to ensure that we get all the nutrients we need, surprisingly, there are no clear guidelines to identify what actually constitutes a low-fat diet.

When it comes to research, most clinical trials seem to classify a low-fat diet as one in which fat provides anything from 20 to 30 per cent of calories. Indeed, in weight-loss trials, a fat restriction in this range seems to be more effective at shifting the pounds than a very low fat intake, where fat provides fewer than 20 per cent of calories. This is probably because diets that are extremely low in fat tend to be too restrictive and boring for most people, with the result that they give up easily. Furthermore, research shows that overweight people who have 20 to 30 per cent of their calories from fat, are more likely to keep the weight off in the long term.

So, if most health experts agree that a low-fat diet is one where around 20 to 30 per cent of calories come from fat, what does this mean in practice? The table overleaf shows the maximum number of grams of fat to aim for depending on different calorie intakes.

Daily calorie intake	Recommended intake of fat grams where...		
	...20% of calories come from fat	...25% of calories come from fat	...30% of calories come from fat
1,250	28	35	42
1,500	33	42	50
1,750	39	49	58
2,000	44	56	67
2,250	50	63	75
2,500	56	69	83

A word about the under-5s

It's important to encourage good eating habits in children as soon as possible. However, health experts agree that low-fat diets are unsuitable for most children under the age of five because they can provide insufficient calories and nutrients for growth. Because young children only have small tummies, they don't physically have room to eat large amounts. This means that meals and snacks need to be packed with calories and nutrients. Fat can make an important contribution to these calorie needs, as well as providing essential fatty acids and fat-soluble vitamins.

That's not to say children should be given high-fat, nutrient-poor foods such as chocolate, biscuits and cakes to boost their calorie intake. Instead, they should get their fat and calories from nutrient-rich foods such as full-fat milk (children under the age of two shouldn't be given skimmed, 1% or semi-skimmed milk), meat, eggs, cheese and oil-rich fish. As children approach school age, they should gradually move towards eating a diet that's based on healthy eating guidelines and, by the age of five, their diet should be low in fat, sugar and salt and high in fibre, with five fruit and veg a day – just like adults.

Guideline Daily Amounts

To help people make sense of the nutrition information on food packs and put it in the context of their own diet, many manufacturers now label their products with Guideline Daily Amounts (GDAs). These are based on dietary requirements for calories and certain nutrients needed for a balanced, healthy diet. GDAs for fat, saturates, sugars and salt are maximum amounts, so it doesn't matter if less than this is consumed (bear in mind that GDAs for fat are based on preventing disease rather than meeting the requirements of a low-fat diet). Others, for example fibre, are based on the amount a person should aim to meet. Quite simply, the amount of a nutrient contained within a typical serving of the food is compared to the GDA and then expressed as a percentage. For example, if a ready meal contains 20g fat, this is compared to the GDA of 70g fat for women or 95g fat for men, revealing it provides roughly 29 per cent of the GDA for a woman and 21 per cent of the GDA for a man. GDAs have been developed for healthy adult men and women of normal weight and also for boys and girls of different ages. The chart below shows the GDAs for men, women and adults (GDAs for adults are based on the values for women and were developed because some packaging only has room on the pack to include one set of values).

Guideline Daily Amount		
	Women/Adults	Men
Calories	2,000	2,500
Fat (g)	70	95
Saturates (g)	20	30
Total sugars (g)	90	120
Fibre (g)	18	18
Sodium (g)	2.4	2.4
Salt (g)	6	6

So how much fat are we eating?

While there is no doubt in the Western world that most people eat too much fat, particularly saturates, the good news is that values have been dropping gradually over the past decade. The UK is a prime example. Figures from the National Diet and Nutrition Survey published in 2001 revealed that adults were getting 33.3 per cent of their calories from fat. The most recent survey published in 2010 found this figure had dropped to 32.9 per cent, just within current guidelines. Nevertheless, intakes of saturates remain too high, with adults currently getting 12 per cent of their calories from this nutrient compared to the recommended maximum of 10 per cent.

Sadly, the figures are less encouraging for children and teenagers. While fat intakes have certainly dropped in the past decade, on average boys still currently get 34 per cent of their calories from fat, and girls 35.2 per cent – considerably more than the recommended maximum of 33 per cent. Saturated fat intakes are even more of a problem, with children and teenagers having, on average, about 13 per cent of their calories from this nutrient.

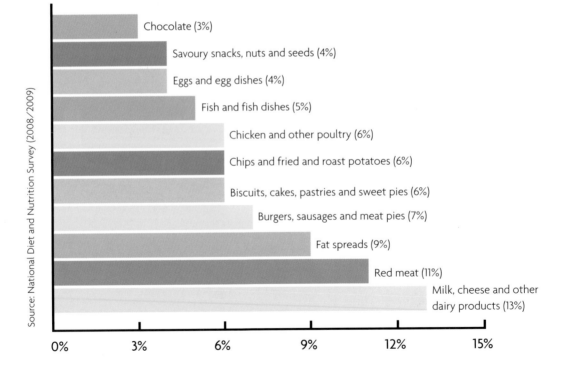

The main sources of fat in our diet

Source: National Diet and Nutrition Survey (2008/2009)

- Chocolate (3%)
- Savoury snacks, nuts and seeds (4%)
- Eggs and egg dishes (4%)
- Fish and fish dishes (5%)
- Chicken and other poultry (6%)
- Chips and fried and roast potatoes (6%)
- Biscuits, cakes, pastries and sweet pies (6%)
- Burgers, sausages and meat pies (7%)
- Fat spreads (9%)
- Red meat (11%)
- Milk, cheese and other dairy products (13%)

0%   3%   6%   9%   12%   15%

Myth makeover

The myth: A fat-free diet is even better than a low-fat diet.

The makeover: It's difficult to follow a fat-free diet since most foods, even fruit and veg, provide small amounts of fat. Meanwhile, we actually need some fat in our diet. Fat helps to insulate the body and small amounts around the major organs help to protect them. Certain components of fat are also important for making hormones, and are an essential part of our cells. Plus, fat-soluble vitamins A, D, E and K are mainly found in foods that contain fat. Furthermore, two fatty acids – linoleic acid and alpha-linolenic acid – can't be made by the body and so must be supplied in the diet. Known as essential fatty acids, these are needed in small amounts for growth, healthy skin and to protect against certain diseases. Ultimately, a fat-free diet equals a very low intake of fat-soluble vitamins and essential fats. The truth is that a fat-free diet is simply not palatable, so most people find it impossible to follow in the long term. It's good news then that it's better to opt for low-fat than to go fat-free.

Eating the right type of fat

Even low-fat diets should still provide sufficient fat to make up 20 to 30 per cent of calories – that's anywhere between 44g and 67g fat for a woman and anywhere between 56g and 83g fat for a man. That's still a significant amount, so it's important that you choose healthier fats.

There are three main types of fat in food – saturates, monounsaturates and polyunsaturates. Most foods contain a mixture of these, but are generally classified according to the type of fat found in the largest amount. In addition, some foods contain trans fats.

Eating healthily is not only about watching your total fat intake, it's also about the balance of fats in your diet. As a first step cutting back on saturated fat is the best way to limit total fat intake. The next step would be to swap some of the saturated fat in your diet for healthier fats such as those from mono and polyunsaturated sources. This is vital as foods rich in these unsaturated fats help to protect us from conditions such as heart disease and diabetes. Here's the low-down...

Saturated fats

A diet high in saturates is proven to increase levels of LDL or 'bad' cholesterol in the blood, one of the risk factors for heart disease. That's why health experts recommend eating fewer foods that are rich in saturates, such as fatty meats, full-fat dairy products, butter, lard, cream, cheese and many processed foods and takeaways.

Polyunsaturated fats

Polyunsaturated fats are divided into two groups – omega-3 fats and omega-6 fats.

Omega-3 fats are divided into short- and long-chain types, both of which help to lower levels of LDL. Short-chain omega-3 fats are found in flaxseed, rapeseed oil, walnuts and green, leafy veg. The body converts short-chain omega-3s into long-chain omega-3s, but this conversion process isn't very efficient. In contrast, oil-rich fish such as mackerel, salmon, pilchards, sardines, trout, kippers, herring and fresh tuna is a naturally rich source of 'ready-made' long-chain omega-3 fats – and it's particularly these types of omega-3s that are linked to keeping the heart beating regularly, making the blood less sticky so that blood clots are less likely and lowering levels of triglycerides (a type of blood fat).

Omega-6 fats are found in pure vegetable oils and spreads such as sunflower, corn, grapeseed and soya oils and margarines, as well as nuts and seeds. These fats lower 'bad' cholesterol but also slightly increase levels of HDL or 'good' cholesterol, the type that helps to protect against heart disease.

Monounsaturated fats

These have a double-whammy effect on cholesterol levels. As well as lowering LDL cholesterol, they also raise HDL cholesterol. Good sources include olive oil, rapeseed oil, avocados, nuts and seeds.

Trans fats

Trans fats are created from hydrogenated fats or hydrogenated vegetable oils, which are sometimes used as an ingredient in processed foods in order to extend their shelf life. They're even more harmful to heart health than saturates because as well as increasing LDL cholesterol they also lower HDL cholesterol. In America, products are labelled with the amount of trans fats they contain, but in the UK, this is uncommon. To see if a food contains trans fats, you need to look at the ingredients. If a product contains hydrogenated vegetable fat or oil as an ingredient, it will almost certainly contain trans fats – and the higher up the list the ingredient appears, the more trans fats the product will contain. In general, hydrogenated vegetable fats and oils are found in cakes, biscuits, margarines, takeaways, pastry, pies and fried foods – although in the UK there's good news as many manufacturers have removed them from their products.

Choosing a low-fat diet

Over the coming pages, you'll find stacks more detail on the best foods to choose (and avoid) to help you stick to a low-fat diet. Nevertheless, looking at food labels is one of the easiest ways to identify whether or not a food contains a little or a lot of fat. Any food that contains 3g fat or less per 100g is low in fat. Products with 20g fat or more in 100g are high in fat.

Be a supermarket sleuth

As well as providing detailed nutrition information, many products also include additional information on the packaging to help us make healthier choices. Here's what some of these claims mean (manufacturers have to abide by these definitions by law, so you can be confident claims are correct if they appear on a product):

- Low-fat – foods must contain 3g of fat or less per 100g, while fluids must contain 1.5g fat or less per 100ml (the exception is 1.8g fat per 100ml for semi-skimmed milk).
- Fat-free – foods or fluids must contain 0.5g of fat or less per 100g or per 100ml.
- Reduced fat – the food must contain 30 per cent less fat than a similar standard product. This doesn't mean the product is low-fat though!
- Low saturates – the total of the saturated fat and trans fats in the product must be 1.5g or less per 100g for food and 0.75g per 100ml for fluid.
- Saturates-free – the total of the saturated fat and trans fats in the product must be 0.1g or less per 100g or per 100ml.
- Light or Lite – this has to follow the same rules as 'reduced' and the product must outline the characteristics that make it light or lite, for example, a reduction in fat or saturates.

Your essential guide to cutting down on fat

Red meat

Red meat has come under attack in the past few decades for its high fat – and particularly saturated fat – content, and it's easy to see why. According to the most recent National Diet and Nutrition Survey, red meat provides 11 per cent of the fat in our diet, with burgers, sausages and pies providing an extra 7 per cent. The good news is that you don't have to give up red meat altogether to follow a low-fat diet – and yes, you did read that correctly!

Thanks to modern feeding programmes, which breed leaner animals, and new butchery techniques that remove more fat, red meat is now leaner than it's ever been. For example, the fat content of pork has dropped from 30 per cent in the 1950s to just 4 per cent today. Meanwhile, lean beef is now as low as 5 per cent fat, and lamb 8 per cent fat.

Better still, while most of us think that red meat is packed with artery-clogging saturates, around half the fat is actually heart-healthy monounsaturates, particularly oleic acid – the same type of fat found in olive oil.

As a result, it's easier than ever to continue enjoying red meat, while keeping fat intakes down. Nevertheless, it's important to choose cuts wisely. For example, while lean pork is just 4 per cent fat, belly pork contains five times that amount. Similarly, lean beef is just 5 per cent fat but regular mince is 16 per cent fat. The golden rule is to look at the nutrition information on the packaging before buying – and if you prefer to buy from a butcher, get him to trim as much fat off as possible. Then don't go and ruin all your hard work by cooking it in loads of oil – opt for low-fat cooking methods instead.

Meat products such as sausages, bacon and cured meats are generally all much higher in fat (and also salt) than fresh meat, so it's wise to steer clear of these. The one exception is cooked ham, which often has the lowest fat content of all popular meats, although it's still high in salt.

If you fancy a change from beef, lamb or pork, veal and game such as venison both contain less than 2 per cent fat and so are excellent choices. Rabbit, with just under 6 per cent fat, contains slightly more fat than lean beef.

It's also important to control portions. Many of us continue to eat large amounts of red meat – often double the amount health experts recommend. In fact, a suitable portion of meat should fit into the palm of your hand or be the same size as a pack of cards.

Cut the fat

Tips for enjoying red meat

- Choose the leanest cuts of meat you can find – most pre-packed meat these days includes nutrition information so check the fat content before putting it in your trolley.
- If you buy meat from a butcher, ask for it to be trimmed to remove any visible fat. Or for pre-packed meat, trim it yourself – this is particularly important if you love the fat on bacon or a pork chop. If it's not there, you won't be tempted to eat it!
- Make lean pork your meat of choice – it contains less fat than beef or lamb.
- Try venison or veal for a change – but don't add loads of fat to cook them.
- Go for trimmed back bacon, which is around 7 per cent fat, rather than streaky bacon with 24 per cent fat!
- Check the fat content of minced beef before you buy – it can vary dramatically from around 5 per cent fat, for extra lean mince, up to 17 per cent fat for regular mince.
- Cut back on portion sizes – around 100g per person is more than enough – and add extra vegetables or beans to boost the quantity of dishes.
- Don't add extra fat to meat when you cook it – investing in a decent non-stick frying pan or wok means you will be able to cook many types of meat without the need for oil.

- Use cooking methods that don't require fat, such as grilling, griddling, baking, casseroling or pot roasting.
- Marinate lean meat before cooking it to add flavour and keep it moist while it cooks.
- Avoid the need to 'seal' a joint of meat (when it's fried in oil before roasting) by placing it into a very hot pre-heated oven for 15 minutes at the start of cooking. The high temperature will 'seal' the meat without you having to add any oil. Then, after 15 minutes, turn the oven temperature down to your regular cooking temperature.
- Don't be fooled into thinking that premium sausages are lower in fat – they're often bigger and contain more meat than cheaper varieties so actually have more fat. Even reduced-fat sausages usually contain significant amounts of fat. For example, a premium sausage can contain 11g fat, while a regular sausage contains 8g fat and a reduced-fat sausage 6g fat.
- Skip cured meats such as chorizo, polony, salami, pepperoni and mortadella – all the little white blobs you can see are fat. Chorizo, for example, can easily contain more than 40 per cent fat, while salami usually contains in excess of 30 per cent fat.
- Ham can be a good choice for including in a low-fat diet but it's important to choose carefully. Many cooked hams can contain as little as 3 per cent fat. Proscuitto, on the other hand, may contain 15 per cent.

Poultry

Chicken and turkey are both thought of as lower-fat alternatives to red meat – and indeed they can be. However, a study conducted by the Institute of Brain Chemistry and Human Nutrition at London Metropolitan University in 2005 found that chicken has got fattier in the past 35 years: in 1970, a chicken was found to contain around 9 per cent fat, compared with 23 per cent fat in 2005. The reason, scientists believe, is that chickens roam less and are given artificial feed. Even organic chickens, which have more room to move about but still don't have to search for their own food, were found to contain 17 per cent fat.

So, with this in mind, when it comes to selecting poultry, it's just as important to choose as wisely as you would with red meat. The most important rule is to cook poultry without the skin, remove any visible fat, and avoid cooking with extra fat. But you can also cut down on fat further by opting for the white breast meat rather than the darker meat – raw chicken breast contains just 1 per cent fat, whereas dark meat contains just under 3 per cent fat.

Meanwhile, don't be tempted to choose duck or goose instead – both are very fatty. Duck, for example, contains six times more fat than chicken breast.

8 smart swaps				
Swap this	g fat	For this	g fat	Save this amount of fat
1 grilled rasher of streaky bacon (20g)	5g	1 grilled lean rasher of back bacon (25g)	3g	2g
100g raw regular mince	16g	100g extra-lean mince	10g	6g
1 grilled premium sausage (50g)	11g	1 grilled reduced-fat sausage (40g)	6g	5g
100g lean roast leg of lamb, well done*	9g	100g lean roast leg of pork, well done*	5g	4g
100g raw dark turkey meat	3g	100g raw turkey breast	1g	2g
125g grilled sirloin steak, well done*	12g	125g grilled rump steak	7g	5g
4 small thin slices salami (20g)	8g	1 slice lean ham (23g)	1g	7g
1 roasted chicken leg quarter with skin (190g)	32g	1 grilled skinless chicken breast (130g)	3g	29g

*The longer you cook meat for, the more fat drips out so well done usually has less fat than rare.

Fish

Health experts recommend that we eat two portions of fish each week, one of which should be an oil-rich fish such as salmon, mackerel, sardines or trout. But they don't recommend that you eat it smothered in batter and fried in oil! All white fish and shellfish such as crab, prawns and mussels tend to be great low-fat options but, as the name suggests, oil-rich fish are much higher in fat. The good news is, as we've already mentioned, oil-rich fish contain heart-healthy omega-3 fats, so it's important to include these types of fish even when you're cutting down on the total amount of fat in your diet.

What's most important is how you cook fish. Serve a 100g fillet of baked cod and you'll have just 1g fat. But take that same piece of cod, dip it in batter then pop it into the deep fat fryer and you'll have 15g fat! Fortunately, fish lends itself to many low-fat cooking methods including baking, grilling, steaming and poaching, so it's easy to add variety to your meals.

Meanwhile, if you're a fan of canned fish, opting for varieties in spring water rather than oil will keep the fat content down – canned tuna in oil, for example, contains 15 times more fat than canned tuna in water!

As for processed products such as ready-prepared breaded or battered fish, fish cakes or fish fingers, always check the nutrition information on the packaging first. Remember, only foods with 3g of fat or less per 100g are considered to be low-fat products. Most breaded fish contain more than 3g fat per 100g, but there are a few exceptions.

A diet rich in fish oils is particularly important following a heart attack. The British Heart Foundation recommends eating 2–3 portions of oily fish a week post heart attack.

Some oil-rich fish contain more fat than others. For example, mackerel contains more fat than salmon, which in turn contains more fat than trout. Similarly, steamed salmon contains around three times more fat than canned salmon.

How much fat is in my fish? (per 100g raw)

Monkfish	less than 1g	Squid	2g	Fresh tuna	5g
Prawns	less than 1g	Plaice	2g	Rainbow trout	5g
Haddock	less than 1g	Halibut	2g	Sardines	9g
Mussells (in shells)	less than 1g	Seabass	3g	Salmon	12g
Cod	less than 1g	Red mullet	4g	Herring	13g
Pollock	less than 1g	Brown trout	4g	Mackerel	16g
Lemon sole	1g	Swordfish	4g		
		Smoked salmon	5g		

Going for canned?

Fat content per 100g (canned and drained where appropriate)

Crab in brine	less than 1g	Sardines in brine	10g
Tuna in brine	less than 1g	Sardines in tomato sauce	10g
Pink salmon in brine	7g	Sardines in oil	14g
Red salmon in brine	8g	Herring in tomato sauce	14g
Pilchards in tomato sauce	8g	Mackerel in tomato sauce	15g
Tuna in oil	9g	Mackerel in brine	18g

Dairy and eggs

With milk, cheese, other dairy products and eggs accounting for roughly a sixth of the fat in our diets according to the latest National Diet and Nutrition Survey, it's not surprising that these foods often come under fire. Fortunately, manufacturers have risen to the challenge set by health professionals and have provided us with a wide range of lower-fat products. And we've certainly embraced them. In fact, we now consume almost four times more low-fat milk than we do full-fat milk.

Milk

While skimmed and semi-skimmed milks have been around for several decades now, the latest addition to our supermarket shelves is 1% milk. As the name suggests, this contains just 1g fat per 100ml and is effectively a half-way option between skimmed milk, which is virtually fat-free, and semi-skimmed milk, which contains just under 2g fat per 100ml. All three options are a better alternative to whole or full-fat milk, which contains just under 4g fat per 100ml, and to Guernsey or Jersey milk, which has a much higher fat content – up to 15g fat per 100ml. And the good

news is that all of these can be used in cooking in the same way you would use full-fat milk.

As for variations on a standard pint, organic and goat's milk is now widely available in skimmed, semi-skimmed and whole or full-fat varieties. Even lactose-free milks may come in semi-skimmed as well as whole varieties. Soya milk can have varying levels of fat and isn't described as skimmed or semi-skimmed, so check the label.

Myth makeover

The myth: Low-fat milk contains less calcium than full-fat milk.

The makeover: Most people are surprised to learn that skimmed, 1% and semi-skimmed milk actually contain slightly more calcium than full-fat varieties. This is because calcium is found in the watery part of the milk and not the creamy part. As a result, when the cream is removed to cut fat, calcium intakes aren't affected.

Cheese

Cheese is generally considered to be off-limits when you're cutting down on fat, but low-fat varieties do exist. Cottage cheese, Quark, ricotta and low-fat soft cheeses are perfect for using in cooking to add a creamy texture, and for using in sandwiches and wraps in place of hard cheeses.

Tips for enjoying cheese

- A small amount of hard cheese looks a lot more when it's grated, especially if you use the finest grating option.
- Go for extra mature Cheddar rather than mild varieties – you won't need to use as much to get the same cheesy flavour.
- Similarly, swap regular hard cheeses for blue-veined cheeses – they contain similar amounts of fat but blue cheeses tend to have a much stronger flavour so you won't need to use as much.
- Use less cheese in sauces and instead grate a little Parmesan on top of dishes – your taste buds will be fooled into thinking the dish is loaded with cheese.
- Try reduced-fat varieties of cheese – many now melt just as easily as full-fat varieties and so are perfect for cooking with.
- Swap Cheddar for other varieties of cheese that are naturally lower in fat.
- Keep portions of cheese small – health experts say a piece around the size of a small matchbox (30g) counts as one portion. We should aim to have three portions of dairy a day, for example 200ml of skimmed milk, a small pot of yogurt and 30g of cheese.

How much fat is in my cheese? (per 100g)

Many of these varieties now come in reduced-fat options so check the packaging to compare the fat content.

Quark	0g	Brie	27g	Wensleydale	32g
Cottage cheese	4g	Danish Blue	29g	Cheddar	33g
Ricotta	11g	Parmesan	30g	Roquefort	33g
Feta	20g	Emmental	30g	Red Leicester	34g
Mozzarella	20g	Gouda	31g	Blue Stilton	34g
Camembert	23g	Lancashire	31g	Cream cheese	48g
Edam	25g	Caerphilly	31g		
Goat's cheese	26g	Cheshire	31g		

What is Quark?

Quark is a soft cheese that's similar to natural fromage frais in terms of its flavour. It has the advantage of being completely fat-free, making it a great alternative to cream cheese in cooking.

Yogurt and fromage frais

Yogurt and fromage frais come in a startling number of varieties so it can be difficult to know what to choose – but you really do need to know what to look for because the variations in fat content can be equally startling. As a rule, you can't go wrong if you look for 'fat-free' on the label – products described as this will contain virtually no fat. Products labelled as 'low fat' are also a good option as they are guaranteed to contain less than 3g fat per 100g. Otherwise, it really is important to check out the nutrition information on the packaging. Greek yogurt might seem like a healthy option, but while fat-free and low-fat varieties exist, unless you check the label, you could end up with a product that contains 10 per cent fat.

Flavoured varieties of low-fat yogurt and fromage frais have never been more popular for a quick and easy pudding. Natural yogurt, while tasty on cereal and mixed with fresh fruit, also makes a great alternative to cream or mayo in dishes. In cold dishes such as coronation chicken, dips and salads, low-fat natural yogurt can simply be used in place of mayo. In heated dishes, however, it's best to use yogurt with a higher fat content rather than low-fat yogurt, as the small amount of fat helps to keep it stable and stops it from separating. Even with a higher fat content, it's still a far better option than cream – a 150g pot of whole milk natural yogurt contains around 5g fat, whereas the same quantity of single cream contains 29g fat and double cream.

How to use yogurt in sauces

Start by making sure that the sauce is quite well reduced because adding yogurt will make it watery again (unlike cream, which thickens the longer you leave it). Then add one teaspoonful of cornflour to a 150g pot of whole milk natural yogurt – this will help to prevent the yogurt from separating once it's heated and will also thicken the sauce slightly.

Take the pan off the heat and leave to cool very slightly, then gradually beat the yogurt into the sauce a tablespoon at a time. Return to a low heat and bring the dish to a gentle simmer for one to two minutes to cook the cornflour and thicken the sauce. Perfect for stroganoff, pasta sauces and creamy curries.

Eggs

Depending on size, an egg contains around 6–7g of fat, so it's not exactly a low-fat product. But that's not to say that eggs can't be enjoyed as part of a nutritious, low-fat diet. Eggs lend themselves to plenty of different low-fat cooking methods such as poaching, boiling, baking and scrambling, so there's really no need to add extra fat to them. Meanwhile, when it comes to using eggs in cooking, there's an easy way to cheat to lower the fat content. All the fat is in the yolk, while the egg white is actually fat-free. This means that it's easy to reduce the fat content of baked dishes and omelettes by replacing some of the whole eggs for egg whites. Hollywood celebs may go all the way and have omelettes made totally from the whites (and there is a recipe for this on page 40) but to keep the consistency and taste, it's usually better to include some whole eggs. As a general rule, swap one whole egg for two whites. So, for example, if a cake requires three whole eggs, replace this with one whole egg and four egg whites to save around 13g fat.

Myth makeover

The myth: Eggs are packed with cholesterol so should be avoided.

The makeover: Eggs (like prawns, crabs, lobsters, cuttlefish, squid, octopus and liver) are certainly higher in cholesterol than many other foods. As a result, in the past, health experts recommended eating fewer of them to keep blood cholesterol levels in check. However, we now know that it is saturated fat, rather than cholesterol in food that has a greater impact on blood cholesterol levels. That's why health professionals now recommend eating fewer foods that contain saturates, such as fatty meats, whole milk, butter, lard, cream, pastry, cakes and biscuits. Meanwhile, health organisations such as the British Heart Foundation and HEART UK no longer say it's necessary to limit eggs, unless you've been advised to do so by a health professional.

Cream

Here's the bad news – all traditional creams are high in fat so it's best to avoid them completely. Lower-fat, reduced-fat and half-fat varieties are certainly better options if you have to use cream, but this doesn't automatically mean that they are low in fat. Light versions of double cream, for example, may still contain around 25 per cent fat. As explained before, if you want a creamy taste then yogurt or fromage frais can often be used instead.

How much fat is in cream? (per 100g)

Single cream	19g
Soured cream	20g
Crème fraîche	40g
Whipping cream	40g
Double cream	54g
Clotted cream	64g

Myth makeover

The myth: Crème fraîche is healthier than cream.

The makeover: It might sound healthier, but with up to 40 per cent fat, it's on a par with whipping cream and contains twice as much fat as soured cream, which it's often used as an alternative to. Lower-fat varieties are available but still check the label.

Fats and oils

There's no getting away from it, but fats and oils are all high in fat, including reduced-fat spreads. All oils, whether olive, rapeseed, sunflower or corn oil, are 100 per cent fat – it's the type of fat that differs among them. Olive oil and rapeseed oil, for example, have a high proportion of monounsaturated fats, while sunflower and corn oil are richer in polyunsaturated fats. It's certainly better to opt for these oils rather than hard fats, which tend to be much higher in artery-clogging saturated fats. But to follow a low-fat diet, you still need to watch the quantity you use. And if you're not convinced, it's worth remembering that just one tablespoon of any oil contains 11g fat!

Most oils are predominantly rich in heart-healthy polyunsaturated and monounsaturated fats, but the exceptions to this are palm oil, which contains around 45 per cent saturates, and coconut oil, which has around 85 per cent saturates.

Hard fats are not only high in total fat, but they are also loaded with saturates. Lard, dripping and ghee (clarified butter), for example, are almost 100 per cent fat, but more than half of the fat in dripping, two-thirds of the fat in ghee and 40 per cent of the fat in lard, is saturated fat. Butter is 82 per cent fat, with two-thirds of this being saturated fat – adding just one teaspoonful to your toast will add 4g fat.

Margarines and spreads can vary considerably in their fat content from brand to brand, ranging from around 55 to 80 per cent fat. The same goes for reduced-fat and 'light' spreads. They are certainly a better option for helping to cut down on fat, but it really is worth checking the nutrition information on the packaging as they can vary dramatically from around 15 to 40 per cent fat.

Finally, it's best to avoid using suet in dishes. Beef suet is around 82 per cent fat and even lower-fat versions of vegetable suet contain around 60 per cent fat.

Ways to use less oil

- Always measure oil used for cooking with a teaspoon or tablespoon. Pouring straight from the bottle means you'll end up using more.
- Use non-stick pans – you won't need to use as much oil in cooking.
- Use a spray oil – 10 sprays provides around 1g fat. If you don't want to use an off-the-shelf spray, invest in a spray canister and fill it with your favourite brand of oil.
- Always wait until oil is hot before adding ingredients. Food absorbs far more oil if it's only lukewarm.
- Keep ingredients like vegetables and potatoes in larger pieces – the smaller they are, the greater the surface area they have and so the more oil they will absorb.
- Spray ingredients like meat, fish and chicken with oil then add to a hot frying pan or griddle – that way you won't end up using more oil than you need.

Starchy foods

Thinking of starchy foods conjures up mostly images of potatoes, pasta, rice, bread and noodles. And it's fantastic news since most of these foods are great low-fat options. Better still, our supermarkets are now stocked with more varieties of low-fat starchy foods than ever before. Sweet potatoes, couscous, bulgar wheat, barley and quinoa help to add variety to our diet so we don't get bored.

But it's important to make sure that we don't undo all the natural low-fat beauty of these products by swamping them with fat. Adding cream, butter or oil to starchy foods massively increases their fat content but adds few nutrients. For example, a 150g serving of potatoes mashed with a little skimmed milk is virtually fat-free, whereas a 150g serving of chips fried in oil contains 10g fat. The golden rule: skip the fat and enjoy carbs neat wherever possible.

Breakfast cereals can also be a good low-fat option, but if they contain nuts and seeds the fat content will be higher, so check the label. Nutty muesli in particular can easily be around 10 per cent fat. Another breakfast option to watch out for is granola. Its healthy image sadly isn't always matched by a healthy fat content – some brands can contain as much as 25 per cent fat as the ingredients are coated in oil before they're baked to form clusters. And always serve cereals with lower-fat dairy products such as fat-free yogurt or skimmed milk.

Bread is another good choice for a low-fat diet providing you don't smother it in butter, marg or low-fat spread. But again, the addition of nuts and seeds will push up the fat content. Ciabatta and other Mediterranean-style breads can also be higher in fat than regular bread as they're often made with olive oil, but it's worth checking the label. Pitta bread, bagels and wraps are a good choice – made even better by the fact that most people don't normally spread them with butter or margarine. Crumpets, teacakes and scones also make good lower-fat snacks (as long as they're not spread with lashings of butter). In contrast, bread products such as croissants, brioches, pastries and muffins are packed with fat, so are best limited.

Finally, the combination of fat and sugar in foods such as biscuits, cakes, doughnuts and puddings might make them taste good, but your waistline and heart won't thank you for it. They are all loaded with fat, much of it saturated.

Fat content of bakery foods (per item)

1 toasted crumpet (40g)	Less than 1g fat	1 fruit scone (48g)	5g fat
1 pitta bread (55g)	Less than 1g fat	1 panini (85g)	5g fat
1 slice wholemeal or white bread (38g)	Less than 1g fat	1 slice fruit cake (60g)	8g fat
		1 individual fruit pie (54g)	8g fat
1 bagel (85g)	2g fat	1 jam doughnut (75g)	11g fat
1 slice ciabatta bread (50g)	2g fat	1 croissant (60g)	12g fat
1 wrap (40g)	3g fat	1 blueberry muffin (72g)	14g fat
1 hot cross bun (50g)	3g fat	1 slice sponge cake with butter cream (60g)	18g fat
1 butter brioche roll (35g)	4g fat		
1 toasted teacake (55g)	5g fat	1 Danish pastry (110g)	19g fat

Fruit and veg

Health experts recommend that we eat five servings of fruit and veg every day to stay healthy and it's good advice. They're packed with vitamins, minerals and antioxidants, provide plenty of fibre to help fill us up, and tend to be low in calories to help us control our weight. But the majority are also low in fat, making them a great choice for a low-fat diet. Of course, there is always the exception, and in the case of fruit and veg, it's avocado. This innocuous-looking fruit is actually loaded with fat – just 1 medium avocado pear contains a massive 28g fat, around 40 per cent of the GDA. It's mainly heart-healthy monounsaturated fat, but if you're cutting down on total fat, then it's best to limit the amount you eat.

Pulses such as peas, beans and lentils are also low in fat and are a great choice to include in a low-fat diet as they help to fill us up. Using them in place of some of the meat in dishes is a really easy way to lower the overall fat content of meals and bulk them up, too, so you don't end up with a tiny portion that leaves you feeling like you're on a diet. Red kidney beans tend to be a popular choice, but it's worth experimenting. Most supermarkets now sell a range of canned pulses including chickpeas, puy and green lentils, and aduki, black eye, borlotti, butter, flageolet, haricot and cannellini beans – good news as you don't have the hassle of soaking dried beans and then cooking them.

Of course, there are still a few things you need to be aware of when selecting veg. Beware of vegetables that are preserved in oil. Antipasti are becoming increasingly popular, but sundried tomatoes, aubergines, courgettes, artichokes, peppers, mushrooms, vine leaves and olives in jars or from the deli counter are often dripping in oil. If you love the Med style of eating, look for veg that come in water or have a go at making your own antipasti by brushing veg with a little olive oil and then cooking them on a griddle or roasting them in the oven. Olives in brine are much lower in fat than those in oil, but they're still salty so go easy on the salt pot for the rest of the day.

Veg and pulse-based dips have a healthy image but hummus can easily contain 30 per cent fat and guacamole around 21 per cent fat. Even reduced-fat versions can have 10 per cent fat or more. Plus, there's the temptation to dip with chips rather than pitta or vegetable crudités. Salsa is a better choice, though the jarred varieties usually contain less fat than fresh ones.

Salads also seem like a healthy option, but if they're smothered with mayonnaise or dressing all that hard work will be undone. Coleslaw, potato salad and Florida salad are among the worst offenders as they're loaded with mayo. Reduced-fat options are usually available, but check the nutrition information as they can vary in fat content considerably.

A word on dressings and mayo

Regular salad dressings and mayonnaises are packed with fat, so it's worth looking for lower-fat alternatives. A tablespoon of mayonnaise contains around 12g fat, with reduced-fat and light versions having around 4g fat, although some brands go even lower than this, with extra light versions that have just 0.5g fat. Tossing salads with dressings can quickly increase the fat content – a tablespoon contains around 7g fat – so always use a spoon to measure them rather than pouring liberally from the bottle. Many brands now do reduced-fat and even fat-free versions of popular dressings so it's worth trying these. Otherwise go with a splash of good-quality balsamic vinegar.

Snacks

It goes without saying that many popular snacks such as biscuits, crisps, savoury snacks, chocolate and other confectionery are loaded with fat and so should be limited on a low-fat diet. In general, the plainer the biscuit, the less fat it contains, so for example, a plain digestive contains around 3g fat while a chocolate digestive contains around 4g fat. A rich tea or jaffa cake has just over 1g fat, and a malted milk or gingernut around 2g fat, so these are the better choices. Cereal bars can contain varying amounts of fat, depending on whether they contain nuts or seeds, so check labels carefully. Flapjacks sound healthy but they can be loaded with fat and also come in large sizes so can easily make a dent in your daily fat allowance.

Crisps and savoury snacks make a significant contribution to fat intakes so follow the golden rules: check the nutrition information, go for the smallest pack size available and limit the number of times you eat these foods. Buying family-size packs or tubs is never a good idea as it's easy to keep on eating them.

Fortunately, there's good news for sweet lovers. Confectionery such as fruit pastilles, traditional Turkish delight, boiled sweets, marshmallows, jelly babies and jelly beans are all fat-free (but they are still loaded with sugar and empty calories so it's wise not to eat too many). Toffees and chocolate on the other hand aren't great choices – and don't be fooled into thinking that dark chocolate is a better option. Toffee contains around 17 per cent fat, while milk, dark and white chocolate all contain around 30 per cent fat.

14 smart snack swaps

Swap this	g fat	For this	g fat	Save this amount of fat
1 large packet of crisps	17g	2 handfuls of home-made fat-free popcorn	4g	13g
2 slices toast with butter	13g	2 slices toast with 2tbsp low-fat soft cheese and 1 tomato	3g	10g
1 small bar of chocolate (50g)	15g	1 banana	0g	15g
Large Danish pastry	25g	Currant bun	4g	21g
Jam doughnut	11g	Iced bun	5g	6g
Ice cream lolly	3g	Fruit lolly	0g	3g
Handful of chocolate-coated peanuts	18g	Handful of chocolate-coated raisins	7g	11g
2 chocolate digestives	8g	2 jaffa cakes	2g	6g
Slice of sponge cake with buttercream filling	18g	Slice of Battenberg cake	4g	14g
Handful of Bombay mix	10g	Handful of Japanese rice crackers	1g	9g
Large chunk of Cheddar with 4 cream crackers	20g	2tbsp low-fat soft cheese on 4 rye crackers	3g	17g
5tbsp garlic dip with a handful of tortilla chips	31g	5tbsp salsa dip with carrot sticks	0g	31g
3 scoops vanilla ice cream	18g	3 scoops lemon sorbet	1g	17g
5 Belgian chocolates	21g	5 marshmallows	0g	21g

Nuts and seeds

Sadly all nuts and seeds are high in fat, with the exception of chestnuts, which are actually low in fat. Yes, it's mainly heart-healthy fat but that's still no good for a low-fat diet. The golden rules are to control portion sizes – easier said than done if you're a nut lover! Going for fresh nuts in their shells helps as it takes longer to get into them, slowing down the speed you nibble. You can also 'dilute' some of the fat by mixing nuts with dried fruit.

Go nuts

Fat content per 100g

Chestnuts	3g	Roasted and salted peanuts	53g	Hazelnuts	64g
Fruit and nut mix	25g	Peanut butter	54g	Brazil nuts	68g
Linseed	34g	Mixed nuts	54g	Walnuts	69g
Pumpkin seeds	46g	Pistachio nuts	54g	Pine nuts	69g
Sunflower seeds	48g	Almonds	56g	Pecan nuts	70g
Cashew nuts	49g	Sesame seeds	58g	Macadamia nuts	76g

Whilst nuts are considered high in fats, many people don't know they are also cardioprotective. This is because of the range of nutrients they provide, including heart-healthy monounsaturated fatty acids, naturally occurring plant sterols, fibre, vitamin E, magnesium, potassium and other naturally occuring plant compounds. So whilst it's important to avoid an excessive intake of nuts they can still be incorporated into recipes and used as snacks as part of a low-fat approach to eating.

Drinks

Surprisingly, it's possible to drink loads of fat! And no, we're not talking about glugging down olive oil! Many fluids are actually loaded with fat, so it's wise to think before you drink. Good fat-free choices include water, of course, and also skimmed milk, pure fruit juices, smoothies and fruit drinks (although do beware that the latter may contain a lot of added sugar). If you can't bear the thought of skimmed milk as a drink, go for 1% or semi-skimmed rather than whole milk – or mix it with fruit to make a shake. Yogurt-based and probiotic drinks can also be a good choice.

With bottles of ready-made milk shakes and drinks, it's always worth checking the label to see how much fat they contain. And avoid shakes from fast-food outlets – a large, healthy-sounding banana or strawberry milk shake can easily contain 14g fat, while a chocolate shake has 15g fat.

Hot drinks aren't usually on the radar when we think about fat, and providing we use low-fat milk in tea or coffee then we really don't need to worry. But if you regularly buy from coffee shops, you may need to think again. A tall cappuccino made with whole milk contains more than 5g fat, while a tall caffé latte has almost 10g. The key is to go 'skinny'. Meanwhile, a hot chocolate with whipped cream can total 26g fat. If you love a chocolate fix, then a mug of homemade drinking chocolate made with skimmed milk is virtually fat-free.

Fortunately, most alcoholic drinks such as lager, cider, wine, sherry and spirits are fat-free (although they're still packed with calories – alcohol contains almost as many calories per gram as fat). However, cream liqueurs are ones to avoid, as are cocktails made with cream or coconut milk.

Making low-fat food taste great

Fat helps to add flavour and moisture to food, so most chefs agree that if you're going to dramatically reduce the fat content of meals then you need to work harder to make food taste great. The good news is that it's very easy to do.

Marinating lean meat, skinless chicken and fish is a great way to add flavour, keep it tender and help prevent it from drying out during cooking. The key is to go for low-fat marinades. In particular, acidic ingredients such as lemon juice, vinegar, wine and yogurt help break down the proteins in meat, tenderising them. But if you're using a marinade that includes an acidic ingredient you'll need to use a glass or ceramic container to stop the food from discolouring. Depending on the size of the meat portion, you can marinate for anything from 20 minutes to several hours, although yogurt marinades are best after 8 hours or overnight.

Rubs and seasoning powders are also a great way to add flavour, although some can be really high in salt, so steer clear of the salt pot if you use them. Most supermarkets now stock a wide selection so get experimenting.

Poaching is a great cooking method for keeping meat and fish moist. Salmon is classically poached in a court-bouillon (a light stock that's usually based on an acidic ingredient such as white wine, vinegar or lemon juice combined with spices). Another flavoursome poaching liquor that goes particularly well with white fish is a mixture of white wine and stock flavoured with lemon and a bouquet garni. But you can also use skimmed milk for poaching fish, especially smoked haddock, and then use the liquor to make a low-fat béchamel sauce. Chicken can also be poached to add variety to your diet. And even red meat such as beef can be poached in red wine mixed with beef stock and herbs.

Meanwhile, it's a good idea to keep your kitchen stocked with a variety of low-fat natural flavour enhancers. Good choices to keep to hand include wine, garlic, citrus juices, pepper, fresh and dried herbs, spices, reduced-salt soy sauce, fish sauce, tomato purée, Worcestershire sauce and a selection of stock options.

Easy tips for cutting fat

- Always eat breakfast – it's the easiest meal of the day to make low fat but do steer clear of fatty baked products such as croissants, Danish pastries and doughnuts.
- Monitor your portion sizes – the bigger the portion the more fat it will contain, so downsize your servings and fill any gaps with veg or salad.
- Swap a couple of meat dishes for veggie dishes each week – you don't need to be a vegetarian to enjoy meat-free meals.
- Include a couple of portions of fish each week – white fish and shellfish are particularly good low-fat choices.
- Grill, griddle, dry roast, bake, poach or steam food, rather than frying or roasting it.
- Trim any visible fat off meat and remove the skin from chicken before you cook it.
- When you're shopping, compare labels and pick products with less fat.
- Choose lower-fat dairy products.
- Put more vegetables and pulses and less meat in casseroles, stews and curries.
- Make meat dishes such as casseroles, Bolognese sauce, stews and curries a day in advance and store in the fridge. Any fat should harden making it easier for you to remove it before reheating.
- Don't use roasting juices to make gravy without skimming the fat off first.
- Measure oil for cooking with a tablespoon, rather than pouring it straight from the bottle.
- If you do choose something high in fat to eat, pick something low in fat to go with it – for example, a jacket potato instead of chips.
- If you're using a moist filling in sandwiches, skip the butter or spread.
- When you do use spread, go for a reduced-fat variety and choose one that is soft straight from the fridge so it's easier to spread thinly.

Breakfasts

All-in-one scrambled eggs and bacon

Per serving

278 cals	6.2g fibre
7.2g fat	1.7g salt
2g saturates	
3.3g sugar	**3g fat per 100g**

Scrambled eggs are always popular, but the days of adding butter and cream will have to remain a distant memory. Here, I've reduced the fat by reducing the yolk content and increasing the amount of white.

Serves 4

2 rashers dry-cure back bacon, rind and
  fat removed, cut into lardons
2 spring onions, finely sliced
8 cherry tomatoes, halved
spray of olive oil
1 x 400g tin white beans, drained
  and rinsed
2 whole free-range eggs + 5 egg whites,
  lightly beaten together
1 teaspoon horseradish cream
2 teaspoons snipped chives
4 thick slices of wholemeal toast

Cook the bacon, onions and tomatoes over a medium heat in a non-stick frying pan with a light spray of oil until lightly softened, about 6–8 minutes. Add the beans and fry for 2 minutes.

Meanwhile, combine the eggs with the horseradish and chives. Season to taste.

Pour the eggs over the bacon and stir to combine, constantly dragging up the edges of the eggs to the centre, producing curds. Once cooked to your liking – I prefer my eggs quite soft – spoon onto the four slices of toast.

Tip

Remember that even after you've turned off the heat the eggs will continue to cook, so work at a brisk pace in the latter stages.

An alternative breakfast fry-up

Per serving

193 cals	3.7g fibre
4.1g fat	2.1g salt
1.2g saturates	
6.8g sugar	**1.3g fat per 100g**

One of my favourite breakfasts, prior to the low-fat era, was crisp bacon with herbed tomatoes and toasted rye bread. Here, I've substituted thinly shaved sandwich ham, which helps control the saturated fat count.

Serves 4

8 vine-ripened tomatoes, halved
    horizontally
spray of olive oil
1 teaspoon soft thyme leaves
3 garlic cloves, peeled
¼ teaspoon sea salt
200g button mushrooms, sliced
1 tablespoon balsamic vinegar
8 basil leaves, ripped
2 tablespoons chopped parsley
175g shaved ham slices
4 slices of your favourite seeded
    bread, toasted

Preheat the oven to 190°C/gas mark 5.

Place the tomatoes, cut side up, in a shallow roasting tray and season with black pepper. Spray with a light mist of oil.

Chop together the thyme, garlic and sea salt until you have a herby paste. In the final stages, this is best achieved by using the back of the knife to crush the mix until very smooth. Spread a little on each of the tomato halves, then place in the oven and cook for 25–30 minutes, checking from time to time. You're looking for the tomatoes to be really soft without collapsing.

Lightly oil a frying pan and cook the mushrooms over a high heat for 5–8 minutes, stirring regularly. Add the balsamic then fold in the herbs and allow to wilt in the heat of the mushrooms. Season well.

Heat the ham (or not) gently and serve with the toast, mushrooms and tomatoes. Warn your team that the tomatoes will be very hot.

Per serving

216 cals	3.1g fibre
4.1g fat	3.5g salt
1g saturates	
6.3g sugar	**1.5g fat per 100g**

Breakfast on rye

Breakfast – so often a neglected meal of the day and it's so important. It's just a case of having a few of the right ingredients to hand: plan your fridge and the rest is child's play.

Serves 1

1 slice of rye bread
1 teaspoon Dijon mustard
45g low-fat cottage cheese
45g sliced smoked salmon
1 tomato, thinly sliced
8 slices of cucumber
1 spring onion, thinly sliced
1 teaspoon lemon juice

Toast the rye bread then spread with the mustard and smooth over the cottage cheese. Next, layer with the smoked salmon, plus a grind of black pepper, followed by the tomato and cucumber slices, arranged in 'scales'. Scatter with the spring onion and drizzle with lemon juice.

Tip

Rye toasts well from frozen and it's great for those on a gluten-free diet.

Mums on the run

Per serving

306 cals   3.4g fibre
1g fat   0.6g salt
0.2g saturates
46g sugar   **0.4g fat per 100g**

Breakfast is definitely an important meal but cereal can get a little dull, so here's a summery alternative.

Makes 1

1 slice of rye bread, or other bread
2 tablespoons 0% fat Greek yogurt
1 banana, cut into chunks
4 strawberries, quartered
¼ teaspoon ground cinnamon
3 teaspoons runny honey

Toast the rye bread. Combine the remaining ingredients and dollop on top of the toast…simple.

Per serving

122 cals   2.7g fibre
1.3g fat   1g salt
0.4g saturates
6.8g sugar   **0.4g fat per 100g**

A gutsy egg-white breakfast

When I was in America, I noticed a trend for egg-white omelettes and, I'll be honest, I thought they must be mad – an omelette with no yolk, therefore no flavour. They were, of course, paranoid about cholesterol in an egg yolk. But we now know that, for many of us, our bodies deal very effectively with dietary cholesterol, and that eggs are not only safe to eat but also one of the original all-round superfoods. There is, however, fat in the egg yolk, so low-fat food should include them sparingly. Here I've developed an egg-white omelette with guts and flavour.

Serves 4

12 free-range egg whites
1 onion, finely chopped
spray of olive oil
115g petits pois, defrosted
2 handfuls of baby spinach leaves, washed
2 tablespoons snipped chives
1 tablespoon chopped parsley
2 tomatoes, deseeded and diced
12 basil leaves, ripped
115g low-fat cottage cheese
3 tablespoons 0% fat Greek yogurt

Whisk the egg whites in a very clean bowl to soft peaks.

Meanwhile, spray the onion with olive oil and cook in a large frying pan over a medium heat until soft but without colour, about 8 minutes. Add the petit pois, spinach, chives and parsley and cook for 2 minutes, stirring constantly, until the spinach has wilted. Fold in the tomato and basil then set aside to cool.

Remove a quarter of the whisked egg white to a bowl, whisk again, then fold in one quarter of the herb and tomato mixture.

Lightly spray a non-stick omelette pan with oil, spoon in the combined egg and herb mixture, then spread evenly and allow to cook over a medium heat until the omelette is golden brown on the bottom. Sprinkle over one quarter of the cottage cheese and yogurt, season with salt and pepper, then fold the omelette to enclose the cheese. Tip on to a warm plate and keep warm while you cook the other three omelettes.

Tip

Some supermarkets now stock pasteurised egg whites in cartons.

Banana bircher muesli

Per serving
227 cals
1.7g fat
0.1g saturates
38.2g sugar

2.9g fibre
0.1g salt

0.7g fat per 100g

Bircher muesli is when you soak your muesli the night before. The contrast of the hot and cold makes this breakfast perfect for a cold morning. When you cook bananas in the skin, you get this wonderful fluffy souffléed effect.

Serves 4

55g toasted oats
180ml apple juice
4 bananas
1 tablespoon runny honey
2 apples, cored and diced
4 tablespoons 0% fat yogurt

Soak the oats overnight in the apple juice.

The next day, preheat the oven to 180°C/gas mark 4.

Place the bananas on a rack in the oven and cook for 20–30 minutes until blackened and very soft when gently squeezed.

Combine the soaked muesli with the honey, apple and yogurt, and spoon a quarter into each breakfast bowl.

Using the tip of a sharp knife, cut down the natural seam of the banana skin and peel back a section of skin. Scoop out the banana flesh with a teaspoon and place on top of the yogurt mixture. Eat while the banana is still hot.

Per serving
286 cals
3.7 fat
0.5 saturates
23.5g sugar

2.5g fibre
0.4g salt

1g fat per 100g

Multi-fibre, multigrain, multi-fruit porridge

Porridge is the perfect way to start your day. This slow-release, fibre-rich food keeps you feeling full until lunchtime, but porridge on its own can be a bit repetitive, so with the addition of other grains and dried fruit it adds a little more texture and lots more flavour.

dry porridge mixture (makes 20 servings)

400g rolled porridge oats
115g rice flakes
115g barley flakes
115g rye flakes
175g millet
1 tablespoon sesame seeds
1 tablespoon linseed
1 tablespoon sunflower seeds
85g sultanas
115g dried apricots, chopped
55g dried cherries
55g dried cranberries
25g goji berries

Mix all the dry ingredients in a large bowl, making sure that everything is evenly distributed. This mixture can be stored in an airtight container, to be used as required.

To cook the porridge for four people, weigh out 225g of the mixture into a bowl, add a pinch of salt, then add 250ml water and 250ml skimmed milk. Stir well, then leave to rest for 15 minutes, which helps all the grains to absorb the liquid. Stir well, then add another 250ml water and 250ml milk.

Bring to the boil over a medium heat, stirring regularly, then reduce the heat and simmer for 12–15 minutes until the mixture is smooth, thick and creamy. Serve with extra milk, a tablespoon of 0% fat Greek yogurt and a teaspoon of brown sugar.

Fruity quinoa

Per serving (based on 6 servings)

331 cals
6.8g fat
0.6g saturates
45.4g sugar

6.4g fibre
0.2g salt

2.8g fat per 100g

Quinoa (pronounced 'keen-wa') has been featuring quite a lot in my diet recently as I've been trying to avoid gluten. It has an interesting, slightly nutty taste with a little chew on the palate. I love it, so give it a shot.

Serves 4–6

175g quinoa, rinsed well and drained
450ml unsweetened orange juice
100g dried figs, chopped
115g dried apple, chopped
115g dried apricots, chopped
40g mixed peel
25g chopped hazelnuts
25g sunflower seeds
grated zest of 1 orange
1 apple, grated
150g raspberries
2 teaspoons chopped mint
4 tablespoons 0% fat Greek yogurt

Put the quinoa and orange juice in a saucepan. Bring to the boil, then reduce the heat and simmer gently for 10 minutes, by which time the liquid should have been absorbed. Cover and leave to cool for 15 minutes.

Tip the quinoa into a bowl and combine with the dried fruits, nuts, seeds, orange zest and grated apple.

Spoon the mixture into four bowls and top with the raspberries and a dollop of fat-free yogurt. Time to eat…

Tip

The cooked quinoa will last 3–4 days in the fridge. Reheat in a microwave then combine with the fruits.

Cucumber mint fizz

Per serving (based on 6 servings)

11 cals
0.1g fat
0g saturates
1.9g sugar

0.5g fibre
0g salt

0g fat per 100g

This is beautifully refreshing, a drink you can enjoy throughout the summer, without getting bored. As a bonus, it is pretty calorie-free.

Serves 4–6

1 cucumber
12 mint leaves
1 teaspoon caster sugar
juice of 2 limes
1.5 litres fizzy water

Using a potato peeler, peel the cucumber into long ribbons continuously until you reach the seeds, then turn the cucumber around and repeat until all you are left with are the seeds.

Place the mint in a mortar or bowl and pound or muddle the mint with the sugar until you have a rough paste. Spoon into a large jug with the cucumber ribbons and the lime juice. This mixture can be made ahead and refrigerated until ready to drink.

Pour on the fizzy water and stir to combine. Pour into ice-filled glasses.

Cosmopolitan breakfast blast

Per serving

162 cals	4g fibre
1.1g fat	0g salt
0g saturates	
17.2g sugar	**0.4g fat per 100g**

There have been many creations on the cocktail front using cranberry juice, but the flavour also suits breakfast fruits really well. An easy way of getting some of your five a day, this concoction can be prepared the night before as most of us are in a rush first thing in the morning.

Serves 4

1 red or pink grapefruit
1 yellow grapefruit
3 navel oranges
1 kiwi fruit
12 mint leaves, shredded
300ml cranberry juice
4 tablespoons toasted oats

Carefully cut all the skin and pith away from the citrus fruits and cut off the skin from the kiwi fruit.

Working over a bowl to catch the juices, carefully cut the citrus fruit between the membranes to obtain segments. Squeeze any remaining juice from the core into the bowl with the fruit. Cut the kiwi in half vertically then cut each half in half again creating four segments, and combine with the other fruits. Fold in the mint and pour in the cranberry juice.

Divide the mixture between four glasses, making sure that each gets one segment of kiwi. Scatter a tablespoon of toasted oats over each serving.

Tip

Feel free to use muesli instead of toasted oats, but beware of the nut content of some mueslis.

My favourite morning pick-me-up

Per serving (based on 3 servings)

145 cals	7.9g fibre
0.8g fat	0.2g salt
0.2g saturates	
33g sugar	**0.2g fat per 100g**

With my own juicer on the market, I've had hours of fun developing different juices: some great, some pretty grim! (I can't get my head around wheatgrass – the 'no pain, no gain' school of thought is not for me.) I keep coming back to this combination, which is a very pleasant drink and undoubtedly does you a great deal of good.

Serves 2–3

2 raw beetroots, washed but not peeled
6 carrots, peeled if not organic
4 dessert apples
1 stick of celery
1 x 10p-size slice of root ginger
ice cubes

Put all the ingredients through your centrifugal juicer on the hard fruit or fast setting. Stir to combine, then pour over ice cubes.

Tip

Beetroot juice should never be drunk in its neat form as the body is a bit overwhelmed by its nutrients. Beetroot is also very hard, so don't push too hard on the plunger.

Blackcurrant breakfast smoothie

Per serving	
262 cals	4.3g fibre
2.9g fat	0.1g salt
0.1g saturates	
27.4g sugar	**0.8g fat per 100g**

Who needs Ribena when you can get masses of vitamin C from fresh blackcurrants? And the oats pack in some good fibre – a slow-release breakfast in a glass.

Serves 4

2 bananas, rough cut
1 punnet of blackcurrants (200g),
    stripped from their stems
115g porridge oats
2 tablespoons runny honey
240ml 0% fat Greek yogurt
300ml skimmed milk
12 ice cubes

Process all the ingredients in your blender and serve in four glasses.

Tip

As long as you use the core ingredients above, you can use any ripe fruits, such as strawberries, raspberries, peaches, apricots and nectarines.

Exotic fruit crush

Per serving	
222 cals	5.7g fibre
1.3g fat	0g salt
0.2g saturates	
48.3g sugar	**0.4g fat per 100g**

This is a lovely breakfast drink, especially good for those lactose who are intolerant. It's very healthy, giving you a fabulous dose of antioxidants.

Serves 4

8 dried apricots, soaked in boiling water
    for 15 minutes then roughly chopped
6 slices dried apple, soaked in boiling
    water for 10 minutes then roughly
    chopped
55g raspberries
2 bananas, roughly chopped
1 mango, peeled, stoned and roughly
    chopped
2 tablespoons wheatgerm
600ml unsweetened apple juice
1 teaspoon roughly chopped mint leaves
10 ice cubes

Place all the ingredients in a blender jug and process until thick and smooth. Pour into four chilled glasses and serve immediately.

Tip

This is a great way to use up what's left in the fruit bowl and at the same time get a valuable dose of healthy ingredients. Play around with different fruit combinations.

Fruit and fibre yogurt layer

Per serving

307 cals 4.7g fibre
2.9g fat 0.4g salt
0.4g saturates
42.6g sugar **1.2g fat per 100g**

This looks a picture, and pictures always mean that your eyes are telling your brain to enjoy it. It's easy to make, colourful, tasty and a great start to your day.

Serves 4

8 strawberries, hulled and sliced, plus 2 for garnish
150g muesli
390ml 0% fat Greek yogurt
2 kiwi fruit, peeled and sliced
1 mango, peeled, stoned and diced
25g dried cranberries
25g dried cherries
2 tablespoons soft dark brown sugar

Divide the strawberry slices between four glasses and top with a little muesli and a dollop of yogurt. Repeat the layers using different fruits each time, finishing with a layer of yogurt. Top with a little brown sugar and some strawberry slices.

Tip

This can be prepared the night before and refrigerated. The brown sugar will melt creating a delicious puddle of sweetness.

Per serving

203 cals 1.6g fibre
8.3g fat 1.6g salt
2.4g saturates
7.2g sugar **2.3g fat per 100g**

Mediterranean vegetable tortilla

This solid, packed omelette is not only good for breakfast but it works well served at room temperature for lunch or supper, and it trebles up as picnic food.

Serves 4

spray of olive oil
2 rashers lean back bacon, cut into strips
4 spring onions, halved lengthways
4 sticks of asparagus, halved lengthways
4 artichoke hearts from a jar (in water), drained on kitchen paper and halved
4 roasted red peppers (not in oil), drained on kitchen paper and halved lengthways
12 basil leaves, ripped
4 free-range eggs
4 egg whites
240ml 0% fat Greek yogurt

Preheat the oven to 160°C/gas mark 2.

Spray a light coating of oil onto the base and sides of a 19cm square cake tin. Line the base and sides with baking parchment paper.

Spray a light coating of oil over a non-stick frying pan, and cook the bacon over a medium heat for 6–8 minutes, then add the spring onions and asparagus and cook for a further 4–5 minutes until lightly softened. Combine with the artichokes and red pepper.

Spoon the mixture into the cake tin, making sure that each 'quarter' has a little of each vegetable, then season and sprinkle with basil.

Whisk the eggs, egg whites and yogurt until well combined then pour over the vegetables. Prod with a fork to ensure that the egg mixture filters down between the vegetables.

Bake in the oven for 35 minutes or until set. Allow to cool slightly before cutting into four squares.

Low-fat ricotta cake with roast tomato

Per serving

127 cals   1.8g fibre

6.1g fat   0.4g salt

2.9g saturates

6.9g sugar   **2.9g fat per 100g**

This is a perfect weekend breakfast, requiring very little preparation and a slow cooking time, and it offers something a little bit different.

Serves 4

spray of olive oil

½ onion, finely chopped

1 garlic clove, finely chopped

2 teaspoons candied peel, roughly chopped

85g frozen leaf spinach, defrosted or 325g baby spinach, washed, cooked and squeezed

115g ricotta cheese

115g low-fat cottage cheese

1 free-range egg, lightly beaten

2 teaspoons chopped dill

⅓ teaspoon grated nutmeg

4 trusses cherry tomatoes on the vine (about six on each)

1 tablespoon sherry or balsamic vinegar

Preheat the oven to 200°C/gas mark 6. Spray four holes of a muffin tray with oil.

Spray a frying pan with a light coating of oil then, over a moderate heat, cook the onion and garlic for 8–10 minutes until soft but not coloured. Add the peel and spinach and cook until any liquid has evaporated, stirring continuously. Allow to cool.

Add the spinach mixture to the two cheeses in a bowl, then stir in the egg and dill. Season to taste. Divide the mixture between the four muffin holes and bake in the oven for 15–20 minutes, until golden.

Meanwhile, place the tomatoes on a roasting tray, spray with oil, season with salt and pepper and cook in the same oven for 12–15 minutes.

Drizzle the sherry or balsamic vinegar over the tomatoes and serve on warm plates with the ricotta cakes.

Soups and snacks

A take on minestrone

Per serving (based on 6 servings)

236 cals	5g fibre
5.7g fat	0.6g salt
1.5g saturates	
8.9g sugar	**0.8g fat per 100g**

This soup has got it all: carbs, protein, loads of goodness and lots of flavour. For even lower fat you can omit the pancetta, but it does give the soup a great flavour. See 'A Different green salad' on page 214 for some info on the edamame beans.

Serves 4–6

1 teaspoon olive oil

55g pancetta, trimmed and finely diced

1 onion, finely chopped

1 leek, washed and finely sliced

3 garlic cloves, finely chopped

1 stick of celery, finely sliced

1 carrot, peeled and finely diced

4 new potatoes, washed, skin on, cut into 1cm dice

1 tablespoon tomato purée

2 sprigs of thyme

2 bay leaves

2 litres fresh chicken or vegetable stock, preferably home-made

1 x 400g tin chopped tomatoes

115g macaroni

85g frozen podded edamame beans

1 x 400g tin flageolet beans, drained and rinsed

150g cauliflower florets

1 large courgette, cut into 1cm dice

115g frozen petits pois, defrosted

12 basil leaves

Heat the oil in a large saucepan, add the pancetta and fry for 3 minutes, then drain off all but one teaspoonful of fat. Add the onion and cook over a medium heat for 8 minutes until starting to soften, stirring from time to time.

Add the leeks, garlic, celery, carrot and new potatoes, stir to combine, then add the tomato purée, thyme and bay leaves, and stir again.

Add the stock and tomatoes and bring to the boil, reduce the heat and simmer for 20 minutes. Add the macaroni and cook for 10 minutes, then add the edamame beans and cook for 2 minutes before adding the flageolet beans, cauliflower, courgette and petits pois. Cook for 4 minutes, then season.

Finally, sprinkle over the basil and serve.

Tip

Obviously, you can vary the vegetables to suit your taste. Just make sure you add root vegetables at the beginning of cooking and any vegetables that grow above ground towards the end.

A gutsy chicken and corn soup

Per serving
296 cals
2.1g fat
0.4 saturates
13.2g sugar

6.2g fibre
1g salt

0.3g fat per 100g

I can't put my finger on why, but there's something magical about the marriage of corn and chicken. This combo has been with us for some time, whether in Chinese cooking or in American chowders – simple, filling and delicious.

Serves 4

1 x 175g boneless, skinless
  chicken breasts
1200ml good chicken stock, preferably
  home-made
1 onion, finely diced
1 carrot, peeled and finely diced
1 stick of celery, finely diced
3 medium floury potatoes, peeled
  and cut into 1cm cubes
2 bay leaves
¼ teaspoon nutmeg
¼ teaspoon sweet paprika
¼ teaspoon ground white pepper
½ teaspoon red pepper, deseeded
  and finely diced
1 x 400g tin puréed (creamed) corn
2 teaspoons reduced-salt soy sauce
180ml skimmed milk
2 teaspoons chopped dill
2 teaspoons chopped parsley

Place the chicken breast in a saucepan with the stock, bring slowly to the boil, reduce the heat and simmer for 8 minutes. Take out the chicken, place on a plate and cover loosely with clingfilm to prevent a dry surface, while it cools. When cool enough to handle either pull the chicken into shreds using 2 forks or cut into small dice, set aside.

Meanwhile add the onion, carrot, celery, potatoes, bay, nutmeg, paprika, white pepper and red pepper to the stock. Bring to the boil, reduce heat and simmer for 15 minutes until the potatoes are cooked.

Stir in the two corns, the soy sauce and the skimmed milk, cook for 3 minutes, stirring without boiling. Finally fold in the chicken and herbs, check the seasoning and serve very hot with bread.

Smoked haddock and potato soup

Per serving
137 cals   0.7g fibre
1.2g fat   1.5g salt
0.2g saturates
8g sugar   **0.3g fat per 100g**

A little bit of Scotland meets India in this slightly bizarre but enjoyable winter soup.

Serves 6

1 onion, roughly chopped
1 stick of celery, roughly chopped
1 carrot, peeled and roughly chopped
2 cloves
2 bay leaves
1 tablespoon curry paste
900ml water
325g undyed smoked haddock
450ml skimmed milk
2 tablespoons mango chutney, diced
   if chunky
325g mashed potato (hot)
juice of 1 lemon
115g low-fat fromage frais
3 tablespoons chopped parsley

Put the onion, celery, carrot, cloves, bay leaves and curry paste in a saucepan with the water and bring to the boil. Reduce the heat and simmer for 15 minutes.

Add the smoked haddock to the pan and cook for 5 minutes. Scoop out the fish and, when it's cool enough to handle, remove any skin and bone and return these (but not the flesh) to the poaching liquor. This should cook for a further 10 minutes before being strained, with the solids discarded. Return the liquor to the saucepan and put it back on heat.

Flake the fish and return it to the stock with the milk and chutney. Bring to the boil, then whisk in the mashed potato to emulsify with the fish and liquid.

Fold in the lemon juice and fromage frais with the chopped parsley. Reheat but *do not boil*. Check the seasoning then serve piping hot.

Chicken, asparagus and noodle soup

Per serving
175 cals   2.2g fibre
1.1g fat   0.1g salt
0.2g saturates
2.3g sugar   **0.2g fat per 100g**

This soup requires a decent home-made stock, if possible, although some of the proprietary brands would do at a pinch (but watch out for the salt levels). This is a light, refreshing meal in a bowl.

Serves 4

1 litre good fresh chicken stock,
   preferably home-made
1 skinless chicken breast, very thinly sliced
3 spring onions, finely sliced
85g frozen petits pois, defrosted
2 teaspoons chopped tarragon
225g fresh asparagus, 2.5cm tips cut
   and the remainder thinly sliced
180ml dry white wine
½ teaspoon crushed garlic
85g thin vermicelli rice noodles
handful of baby spinach

Heat the stock in a large saucepan then add the chicken breast and cook for 1 minute.

Add the spring onion, peas, tarragon, asparagus tips and slices, white wine and garlic, bring back to the boil, then cook for 3 minutes.

Add the vermicelli and spinach and cook for 2 minutes until the noodles have softened and the spinach wilted. Check the seasoning and serve piping hot.

Tip

You could use leftover cooked chicken, instead of raw, if you like.

Crab and coriander soup

Per serving

166 cals   1.5g fibre

9.9g fat   3.7g salt

5.2g saturates

5.1g sugar   **1g fat per 100g**

There's a real earthy blast of heat from the Thai red curry paste in this soup. There's no need to spend fortunes on really good hand-picked white crabmeat, although it would be nice; you'll often find brown and white crabmeat sold separately.

Serves 6

2 teaspoons vegetable or rapeseed oil

1 onion, finely diced

2 tablespoons Thai red curry paste

1 red pepper, deseeded and finely diced

2 garlic cloves, crushed to a paste with a little salt

1 stalk of lemongrass, left whole but bruised all over with the back of a knife

2 lime leaves, left whole

300ml reduced-fat coconut milk

900ml dashi or fish stock

175g brown crabmeat

1 tablespoon anchovy essence

85g frozen petits pois, defrosted

115g fresh or drained canned crab (white meat)

1 tablespoon nam pla (fish sauce)

1 tablespoon fresh lime juice

4 tablespoons chopped coriander

2 red chillies, deseeded and finely sliced

3 spring onions, finely sliced

Heat the oil in a large wok or saucepan, then cook the onion for 6 minutes until starting to soften. Add the curry paste, stir to combine and cook for 1 minute before adding the red pepper, garlic, lemongrass and lime leaves. Stir then cook for 3 minutes.

Add the coconut milk, stock, brown crabmeat and anchovy essence. Bring to the boil, stirring from time to time, and cook for 10 minutes.

Add the peas, white crabmeat and cook for 3 minutes, then add the nam pla and lime juice. Remove the lemongrass and discard.

Top the soup with the coriander, chillies and spring onions.

Cauliflower and rocket soup

Per serving (based on 8 servings)
118 cals
3.3g fat
0.8g saturates

8.6g sugar
3.2g fibre
1.9g salt

0.6g fat per 100g

Cauliflower makes a delicious soup, and with the addition of rocket you get a lovely peppery aftertaste. I've added crunch by including some fast-roasted cauliflower florets.

Serves 6–8

1 tablespoon vegetable oil

1 onion, roughly chopped

2 garlic cloves, roughly chopped

1 stick of celery, thinly sliced

1 carrot, peeled and thinly sliced

1 large floury potato, peeled and thinly sliced

1 large cauliflower (1kg), two-thirds roughly chopped (including the core), one-third cut into small florets

1 bay leaf

½ teaspoon chopped thyme leaves

1 litre good vegetable stock

500ml skimmed milk

1 teaspoon ground cumin

2 handfuls of rocket leaves

½ teaspoon ground white pepper

Preheat the oven to 220°C/gas mark 7.

Heat half the vegetable oil in a large saucepan. Add the onion, garlic, celery and carrot and cook for 8–10 minutes over a medium to low heat to lightly colour and soften the onion. Add the potato and cook until the potato starts to stick and the edges start to soften.

Add the roughly chopped cauliflower, bay leaf, thyme and stock to the pan. Bring to the boil then reduce the heat and simmer for 15–20 minutes. Add the milk and warm through without letting the soup boil.

Meanwhile, toss the cauliflower florets with the remaining oil in a bowl, then add the cumin and toss again. Place in a roasting tray and cook for 12–15 minutes, until the cauliflower begins to brown but still retains some bite.

Process the soup in a blender with the rocket and white pepper – if your soup is very hot, only fill the jug to half, leaving out the stopper in the lid. Blend it in batches, then pass through a fine sieve. Check the seasoning.

Drain the roast cauliflower and divide between hot soup bowls. Pour in the soup and serve immediately.

Hot and sour prawn soup

Per serving
126 cals   1.4g fibre
2.3g fat   5.2g salt
0.6g saturates
11.1g sugar   **0.5g fat per 100g**

Loosely based on that Thai favourite Tom Yum Goong, this soup is something I often knock up for a very light, very healthy lunch. It's a great alternative to creamy soups but still tastes amazing. You can vary the fish if you want. It's equally as good with flakes or chunks of white fish, scallops or oysters. Vary the heat by adding more or less chillies.

Serves 4

1 litre dashi or vegetable stock

1 onion, peeled and grated

3 tablespoons galangal or ginger, peeled and julienned

1 lemongrass stalk, outside leaves removed and bruised with the back of a knife

3 kaffir lime leaves, finely shredded

3 garlic cloves, crushed to a paste with a little Maldon salt

2 bird's eye red chillies, finely sliced then bruised

85g shiitake mushrooms, stalks discarded and caps quartered

12 cherry tomatoes, halved horizontally

12 peeled raw tiger prawns, deveined

small handful (20g) of baby spinach leaves

4 tablespoons brown rice miso

juice of 2 limes

2 tablespoons chopped coriander leaves

1 tablespoon liquid honey

120ml clear apple juice

Heat the stock in a non-reactive saucepan with the onion, galangal, lemongrass, lime leaves, garlic and chillies. Bring to the boil, reduce the heat and simmer for 10 minutes.

Add the mushrooms, tomatoes, prawns and spinach and stir to combine. Cook for 3 minutes, then fold in the miso, lime juice, coriander, honey and apple juice. Serve immediately.

Tip

If shiitake mushrooms are not available, use clean button mushrooms and include the stalks, or look for a nice mushroom selection box.

Lentil, couscous and chilli soup

Per serving

281 cals 4.1g fibre

3.5g fat 0.3g salt

0.5g saturates

6g sugar **0.7g fat per 100g**

I've been a fan of chunky soups ever since I converted to a mainly GI diet. This doesn't mean I'm averse to a smooth soup, it's just that these main-course soups fill you up and, for a meal, are relatively low in calories. This one is low GI, a good source of fibre and has a decent amount of beta-carotene. Serve with warm, seeded bread.

Serves 6

1 tablespoon olive oil

1 onion, roughly chopped

1 carrot, peeled and roughly chopped

1 stick of celery, finely sliced

3 garlic cloves, crushed to a paste
   with a little rock salt

1 tablespoon tomato purée

1 tablespoon rose harissa

2 teaspoons sweet paprika

½ teaspoon chilli powder

300g yellow lentils

55g long grain rice

1 teaspoon cumin

½ teaspoon ground coriander

1 x 200g tin chopped tomatoes

2 litres homemade vegetable stock

55g couscous, soaked in cold water
   for 10 minutes and drained

3 teaspoons chopped mint

1 tablespoon chopped coriander

3 tablespoons chopped parsley

1 red chilli, finely sliced

2 spring onions, finely sliced

2 tablespoons 0% fat Greek yogurt

Heat the oil in a large saucepan over a medium heat, and cook the onion, carrot and celery for 8–10 minutes until softened but without colour. Add the garlic and cook for a further 2 minutes.

Stir in the tomato purée, harissa, paprika and chilli powder and cook, stirring constantly for 1 minute.

Add the lentils, rice, cumin and coriander, and stir to combine, followed by the tinned tomatoes and stock. Cover, bring to the boil, then reduce the temperature and simmer for 35 minutes.

Ladle one-third of the soup into a blender and purée until smooth, then return to the pan and stir to combine. Add the couscous, 2 teaspoons of mint, ½ tablespoon of coriander and all the parsley. Return to the heat.

Meanwhile, combine the remaining herbs with the chilli, spring onions and yogurt, season and mix well.

Serve the soup piping hot in warmed bowls with a floater of yogurt and a wedge of warm seeded bread.

A very quick no-cook pâté

Per serving

105 cals · 0.5g fibre

2g fat · 1.5g salt

0.6g saturates

2.4g sugar · **1.4g fat per 100g**

This pâté has lots of lovely flavours and is a good standby to have in the fridge for when you get those munchy moments – all you need are a few knife skills. Serve with warm bread, crackers, pitta bread, the choice is yours.

Serves 4

1 cooked chicken or turkey breast, skin removed

115g lean cooked ham

55g clean button mushrooms, finely diced

4 cornichons, finely diced

1 tablespoon Lilliput (baby) capers

2 shallots, finely diced

2 tablespoons chopped parsley

juice and grated zest of 1 unwaxed lemon

2 teaspoons anchovy essence or sauce (optional)

1 teaspoon chopped tarragon

120ml low-fat fromage frais

Finely chop the chicken and ham into small dice. You could use a food-processor rather than a knife but this tends to pulp the meat to a paste – I prefer a rougher texture.

Then, it's really simple: just combine the meat with all the other ingredients and mix well. Allow the flavour to develop for one hour before seasoning.

Tip

You can use the same recipe to make a variety of fish pâtés: try using tinned salmon (blend in a food-processor), cooked prawns (dice finely) or white crabmeat (no chopping or blending required, just mixing).

A textured bean pâté

Per serving

96 cals · 2.7g fibre

1.5g fat · 0.2g salt

0.4g saturates

3.8g sugar · **1.1g fat per 100g**

A cross between pâté and a dip, it's a useful store-cupboard standby that has a good balance of flavours.

Serves 6

1 floury potato, peeled and cut into 2cm dice

1 x 400g tin of cannellini beans, drained and rinsed

2 garlic cloves, crushed to a paste with a little salt

2 teaspoons caster sugar

3 tablespoons low-fat fromage frais

3 spring onions, finely sliced

2 tomatoes, deseeded and diced

8 basil leaves, roughly chopped

1 tablespoon sherry vinegar

1 hard-boiled egg, finely chopped

Place the diced potato into a pan of cold water with a little salt and bring to the boil. Simmer until tender, about 10 minutes, then add the drained beans to the pan to warm through. Drain and return to dry out over a low heat.

Add the garlic, sugar and fromage frais to the warm potato and bean mixture and crush the lot with a potato masher, or more slowly with a fork. (It's important to add the wet ingredients while the potatoes are still warm so that they are more easily absorbed.)

Fold in the remaining ingredients and season well. Serve with crackers, or bruschetta or crostini, or with warm pitta breads.

Tip

There are many sorts of tinned beans, all good, but white beans give a better colour.

Chicken satay with cucumber relish

Per stick

72 cals
1.4g fat
0.8g saturates
8.9g sugar

0.2g fibre
0.3g salt

1.7g fat per 100g

There are not many who will turn down a satay stick, they are very moreish but before you help yourself to a third or fourth, always take into consideration the total fat, not the fat per skewer. Peanuts are traditionally used in a satay sauce but this version skips them, which considerably cuts the fat – and also has the advantage of making these skewers suitable for anyone with a nut allergy.

Makes 15 sticks

CHICKEN SATAY:

300g skinless chicken breast, cut
   into thin strips (15)
120ml reduced-fat coconut milk
2 tablespoons runny honey
1 tablespoon light soy sauce
4 tablespoons finely chopped coriander,
   leaf, stalk and root (if available)
2 hot red chillies, finely diced
4 garlic cloves, mashed to a paste with
   a small amount of Maldon salt
1 teaspoon grated ginger
½ teaspoon ground turmeric
½ teaspoon of curry paste (hot)
lime wedges, to serve

CUCUMBER RELISH:

180ml rice or cider vinegar
6 tablespoons runny honey
1 cucumber, peeled, deseeded and
   finely diced
2 teaspoons tamarind paste
3 tablespoons finely chopped coriander
1 teaspoon finely chopped mint
2 mild red chillies, deseeded and very
   finely sliced on the diagonal
1 teaspoon grated ginger

To make the cucumber relish, bring the vinegar and honey to the boil in a non-reactive saucepan, reduce the heat and simmer for 10 minutes. Pour into a bowl, allow to cool then fold in the remaining ingredients. To keep the cucumber green and tangy make it no more than 1 hour before. If you want to make it the day before, the cucumber will lose its bright green colour but the flavours will be developed…you can't have it both ways.

For the satay, combine all the ingredients except the chicken in a bowl, then add the chicken and massage together until the meat is fully coated. Marinate in the fridge for up to 24 hours but for no less than an hour.

To place on (pre-soaked) wooden skewers, weave the stick through the chicken in an 'in and out' broad sewing movement then stretch the chicken down the skewer leaving the sharp point covered with chicken to create a flat surface, top and bottom.

Place the skewers on a very lightly oiled, flat roasting tray and place under a hot grill, cook for 3–4 minutes each side, then serve with the relish, lime wedges, and for a main course, serve with plain boiled rice.

Filo beef rolls

Per serving
325 cals   5.2g fibre
7.3g fat   0.5g salt
2.1g saturates
30.3g sugar   **3g fat per 100g**

Not many of us have access to spring roll wrappers but you can get a similar effect by using filo pastry. The filling is simple, with a slight sweetness given by the fruits. Serve with a sweet chilli dipping sauce and salad.

Serves 4

2 teaspoons olive oil
1 onion, finely chopped
2 garlic cloves, finely chopped
½ teaspoon ground cinnamon
2 teaspoons mint sauce
150g extra-lean minced beef
1 carrot, peeled and finely diced
1 leek, washed and finely diced
6 apricots, finely diced
55g sultanas
55g dried cherries
8 sheets filo pastry
spray of olive oil

Heat the oil in a frying pan, add the onion and garlic and cook over a medium heat for 8–10 minutes. Stir in the cinnamon and mint sauce.

Add the beef mince to the onion, breaking up any lumps with the back of a spoon. Cook until brown then add the carrot, leek, apricots, sultanas and dried cherries. Cook for 12 minutes until the carrots have softened slightly. Allow to cool for 10 minutes.

Preheat the oven to 200°C/gas mark 6.

Lay one sheet of filo on your worktop and cut it in half crossways. Spray one half with oil, turn it over and spray it again; lay the other sheet on top and spray again. Lay one-eighth of the beef mixture along the edge of the filo closest to you, leaving a 1cm border. Fold the ends over the beef, then roll up making sure the ends are tucked in. Lay the roll, seam side down, on a flat baking tray. Repeat the process with the other seven.

Bake for 12–15 minutes until golden, checking from time to time to make sure they are not burning.

Spiced vegetable fritters with mango chutney dip

Per serving	
265 cals	2.5g fibre
3.1g fat	1.8g salt
0.4g saturates	
16.2g sugar	**1g fat per 100g**

This Indian-influenced recipe comes from the same family as an onion bhaji but has more flavour. We're not deep-frying here so have no fear, just enjoy them when you're feeling peckish. They do reheat, although they are better cooked fresh.

Serves 4

150g besan (gram) flour
1 teaspoon salt
120ml water
½ teaspoon turmeric
½ teaspoon chilli powder
½ teaspoon ground coriander
½ teaspoon ground cumin
½ teaspoon garam masala
2 garlic cloves, grated
1 onion, finely sliced
¼ butternut squash, peeled, deseeded and grated
1 courgette, grated
3 new potatoes, grated
3 tablespoons chopped coriander
2 teaspoons chopped mint
spray of vegetable oil

DIP:

3 tablespoons smooth mango chutney
4 tablespoons 0% fat Greek yogurt
1 teaspoon chopped mint

Combine the flour, salt and water in a bowl and beat until smooth. Add the spices and beat again.

Combine the vegetables in a bowl and mix well. Fold in the herbs then pour in the batter and stir to combine.

Spray a large frying pan with vegetable oil, then drop spoonfuls of vegetable batter into the pan, pushing them down to make flat, rough circles. Cook over a medium heat for 4 minutes each side. If you need to cook the fritters in batches, keep the others warm in a low oven.

Make the mango chutney dip by combining all the ingredients, and serve with the fritters.

Tip

There are all sorts of possibilities when it comes to vegetables to use – try a green fritter with broccoli, peas and cooked, chopped spinach.

Bruschetta of roast peppers with chilli, garlic and parsley

Per serving
262 cals
5.1g fat
0.8g saturates
13.2g sugar

4.4g fibre
1.3g salt

2g fat per 100g

The topping can also be eaten as part of an antipasto spread, a salad or folded through pasta. These wonderful, warm Med flavours are packed with antioxidants, especially vitamin C and beta-carotene.

Serves 4

4 red peppers
3 anchovy fillets, halved lengthways
 and rinsed
¼ teaspoon crushed dried red chillies
4 garlic cloves, thinly sliced
3 spring onions, finely sliced
2 tablespoons chopped flat-leaf
 parsley
zest and juice of 1 organic orange
2 teaspoons Lilliput (baby) capers,
 drained and rinsed
2 teaspoons extra virgin olive oil
1 ciabatta loaf, halved horizontally
 lengthways, then each slice
 cut in two

Place the peppers over a gas flame or on the highest shelf under a hot grill. Keep turning with tongs, as each side becomes blackened and blistered. Place the peppers in a bowl and cover tightly with clingfilm and leave for 20 minutes to steam in their own heat. When cool enough to handle, scrape off the blackened skin, remove the calyx and seeds then cut the flesh into long thin strips.

Tip the peppers together with any juices from the bowl into a clean bowl and combine with the anchovies, chilli, garlic, spring onions, parsley, zest and juice of the orange and the capers, season to taste.

Meanwhile, brush the ciabatta slices with a scant amount of olive oil and toast the cut side under the grill or on a griddle pan until golden. Divide the peppers between the four slices and serve as a snack or with a leaf salad.

Tip

To save time buy yourself a jar of wood-roasted peppers, but as they're usually in olive oil, drain well and pat with absorbent kitchen paper. Unfortunately the tinned peppers in brine have little or no flavour.

Spicy pea fritters with coriander and potato raita

Per serving
302 cals
5.4g fat
0.6g saturates
6.5g sugar

2.5g fibre
0.5g salt

1.9g fat per 100g

This dish is loosely inspired by Indian pakoras, which are usually deep-fried. In this case we lightly pan-fry the fritters with the merest hint of vegetable oil. They are extremely moreish and work very well for a light lunch or as a snack to hand round with drinks.

Serves 4

225g gram (chickpea) flour
1 teaspoon bicarbonate of soda
180ml water
2 teaspoons vegetable oil
1 small onion, roughly chopped
4 garlic cloves, roughly chopped
1 teaspoon ground turmeric
½ teaspoon ground cumin
½ teaspoon ground coriander
½ teaspoon ground fennel
½ teaspoon dried chilli flakes
2 teaspoons chopped mint
140g frozen petits pois, defrosted
3 spring onions, finely sliced
handful of rocket leaves, roughly
    chopped
spray of vegetable oil

RAITA:

240ml 0% fat Greek yogurt
175g cooked potato, cut into 1cm dice
½ bunch of coriander, roughly
    chopped
1 garlic clove, crushed to a paste with
    a little sea salt
½ teaspoon cumin seeds, toasted

Sift the gram flour and bicarb into a bowl with a pinch of salt. Whisk in the water to produce a smooth batter.

Meanwhile, heat the oil in a frying pan and, over a medium heat, cook the onion and garlic for 8–10 minutes to soften them with no colour. Add the spices and stir to combine, and cook for a further minute. Allow to cool slightly then blitz the mixture in a mini food-processor until reasonably smooth.

Spoon the spiced onion into the batter along with the mint, peas, spring onions and rocket. Allow the mixture to rest for 15 minutes to let the flavours develop.

Meanwhile, combine all the ingredients for the raita in a bowl, and leave for 30 minutes. Season to taste.

Preheat the oven to 160°C/gas mark 2.

Spray a non-stick frying pan with vegetable oil and warm over a medium heat. Drop level tablespoonfuls of the pea batter into the pan and flatten slightly. Cook for 3 minutes on each side, then place in the oven to keep warm while you cook the remainder in batches. Serve with the raita.

Tip

Have fun changing the content of the fritters, using different vegetables or even oven-cooked chicken or prawns.

Turkey and lettuce cups

Per serving
174 cals
6.7g fat
2.4g saturates
6.8g sugar
1.2g fibre
2.2g salt
2.9g fat per 100g

Every time we go out for a Chinese these lettuce cups are always my kids' first choice. They are light, reasonably healthy and are packed full of flavour and they're pretty quick to make.

Serves 4

2 teaspoons vegetable oil

2 teaspoons very finely shredded lemongrass, outside layers discarded

2 bird's eye chillies, deseeded and finely sliced

3 garlic cloves, crushed to a paste with a little salt

2.5cm piece of fresh ginger, peeled and finely grated, retaining any juice

275g turkey or chicken mince

½ cucumber, deseeded and cut into 1cm dice

55g mangetout, topped and tailed and cut into very thin batons

4 spring onions, thinly sliced on the diagonal

3 water chestnuts from a can, drained and cut into 5mm dice

8 basil leaves

handful of coriander leaves

4 iceberg or little gem leaves

55g beansprouts, soaked in iced water then drained just before use

DRESSING:

juice of 2 limes

1 tablespoon reduced-salt soy sauce

1 tablespoon rice wine vinegar

2 tablespoons kecap manis (Indonesian soy sauce)

2 teaspoons liquid honey

½ teaspoon chilli oil

Heat a wok with the oil, then add the lemongrass, chillies, garlic and ginger and cook for 2 minutes, stirring continuously. Remove and set aside.

Add the turkey or chicken mince to the wok and cook over a high heat, stirring continuously and breaking up any lumps with a fork or spoon. Cook for about 4 minutes until brown.

Whisk together the dressing ingredients.

Return the lemongrass mixture to the wok, along with half the dressing, and toss thoroughly. Add the remaining ingredients, except for the beansprouts and lettuce leaves, and stir-fry for 30 seconds. Tip into a bowl and serve with the remaining dressing.

Your fellow diners then spoon the turkey into their lettuce 'cups', top with bean sprouts and roll up and enjoy the crunch.

Tip

To separate iceberg leaves without tearing them, place the lettuce core-side up on your cutting board, remove the core using a small sharp knife then hit the lettuce hard on the bottom, which will help to loosen the leaves.

Curried aubergine purée

Per serving
86 cals   3.5g fibre
3.2g fat   0.2g salt
0.5g saturates
8g sugar   **1.3g fat per 100g**

I know that aubergines are not everyone's cup of tea but I am a bit of a fan as I find them wonderful vehicles for absorbing some fab flavours. This dish, as well as being a great vegetable side, also doubles up as a dip, or you can serve it with rice.

Serves 6

2 large aubergines
1 tablespoon vegetable oil
2 onions, finely chopped
2 garlic cloves, crushed to a paste
  with a little salt
2 teaspoons grated ginger
2 chillies, finely diced
2 cardamom pods, lightly crushed
½ teaspoon ground cumin
½ teaspoon ground coriander
¼ teaspoon ground fennel
½ teaspoon ground turmeric
½ teaspoon freshly ground black pepper
225ml 0% fat Greek yogurt
1 teaspoon garam masala
3 tomatoes, roughly chopped
2 tablespoons chopped coriander

Preheat the oven to 190°C/gas mark 5.

Place the aubergines on a rack in the oven and cook until very soft and almost collapsed, about 40–45 minutes.

Meanwhile, heat the oil in a large saucepan and cook the onions with the garlic, ginger and chillies over a low heat for 10–12 minutes. Add the five spices (not the garam masala) and cook for a further 3–4 minutes.

When the aubergines have cooked, cut them in half lengthways and scoop out all the flesh, discarding the skins. Chop the flesh and add to the onion spice mixture and cook gently for 5 minutes. Add the yogurt, bring to the boil then reduce the heat and cook for 8 minutes, stirring regularly.

Finally, fold in the garam masala, tomatoes and chopped coriander, cook for 3 minutes and check the seasoning.

Baked herby tomatoes on rye toast

Per serving
220 cals   4g fibre
4.5g fat   1.8g salt
0.7g saturates
6.4g sugar   **1.9g fat per 100g**

Serves 4

6 ripe but firm large tomatoes, cut in half
½ teaspoon salt
2 shallots, peeled and rough chopped
2 garlic cloves, rough chopped
1 teaspoon thyme leaves
2 anchovy fillets, drained and rough chopped
2 tablespoons parsley leaves
2 teaspoons snipped chives
½ teaspoon dried chilli flakes
85g fresh white breadcrumbs
1 teaspoon extra virgin olive oil
4 slices of rye toast

Carefully remove most of the seeds from the tomatoes with a teaspoon or melon baller. Sprinkle the cut sides with salt and place cut-side down on kitchen paper to remove some of the liquid. Leave to stand for 20 minutes.

Preheat the oven to 200°C/gas mark 6.

Place the shallots in a food-processor with the garlic, thyme, anchovies, parsley, chives, chilli flakes, breadcrumbs and oil and pulse until well combined but not a paste. Season to taste.

Spoon the mixture into the tomato cavities, mounding it high, then bake in the oven for 20–25 minutes. Keep an eye on them, for signs of burning, and turn the oven down if necessary.

Serve the tomatoes on the rye toast.

Falafel

Per serving (based on 8 servings)
122 cals
2.4g fat
0.3g saturates

3g sugar
3.1g fibre
1g salt

2g fat per 100g

These can be made using canned chickpeas, but the texture will not be the same as when using dried. Falafel are normally deep-fried, but in the interests of a low-fat diet you can pan-fry them in a small amount of oil.

Serves 6–8

400g dried chickpeas, soaked overnight in plenty of cold water
1 onion, roughly chopped
3 garlic cloves, roughly chopped
2 tablespoons chopped parsley
1 tablespoon chopped coriander
1 teaspoon ground cumin
½ teaspoon ground fennel
1 teaspoon bicarbonate of soda
2 tablespoons plain flour
1 teaspoon salt
spray of oil

YOGURT DIP:
240ml 0% fat Greek yogurt
1 tablespoon chopped mint
1 tablespoon sesame seeds, toasted
1 teaspoon mashed garlic

To make the dip, combine all the ingredients and leave for half an hour for the flavours to develop.

Meanwhile, place the soaked chickpeas with the onion, garlic, herbs and spices in a food-processor and pulse until almost smooth. Tip into a bowl, then add the bicarb, flour and salt and mix well. Turn on to a floured surface and knead for 5 minutes. Place the mixture on some clingfilm and roll up like a sausage, about 4cm in diameter. Leave to rest in the fridge for 30 minutes.

Cut the falafel 'sausage' into 1cm discs.

Spray the oil onto a frying pan and cook the falafel discs in batches over a medium heat for 2 minutes on each side. Keep warm in the oven then serve with the yogurt dip.

Two dips

These dips, to accompany your crackers or crudité vegetables, are made using plenty of store-cupboard ingredients. Each makes roughly 600ml.

CHILLI AND RED PEPPER:

3 roasted peppers from a jar, drained well and patted dry
1 onion, finely chopped
2 tablespoons pickled jalapeño chillies from a jar, drained and chopped
6 basil leaves, finely chopped
1 x 200g tin chopped tomatoes
1 teaspoon tomato purée
225g low-fat cottage cheese

Combine all the ingredients except for the cheese in a blender or food-processor, and blend until smooth. Fold the purée into the cottage cheese and it's ready.

SPICED SPINACH AND YOGURT:

115g frozen chopped spinach, drained and squeezed dry
2 garlic cloves, crushed to a paste with a little salt
1 teaspoon ground cumin
½ teaspoon ground turmeric
1 teaspoon hot or mild curry paste
2 spring onions, finely chopped
2 teaspoons lemon juice
400g 0% fat Greek yogurt

Combine all the ingredients, check the seasoning, and serve.

Potato, tomato and basil rolls

This recipe is multi-purpose, I'm going to cook them in muffin tins, but you could make one loaf or even pan-fry patties.

Makes 8

200g floury potato, peeled and cut into 1cm cubes
30g low-fat spread
300g self-raising flour
250ml skimmed milk
1 roasted red pepper from a jar, drained and diced
85g sun-dried tomatoes, chopped
12 basil leaves, roughly chopped
55g reduced-fat mozzarella, grated

In a pan of boiling, salted water, cook the potatoes for about 10 minutes until tender, then drain and return to the hot pan to dry out slightly.

Meanwhile, preheat the oven to 200°C/gas mark 6.

Mash the potato with the low-fat spread, then sift in the flour and mix to combine. Stir in the milk and fold in the red pepper, tomatoes, basil and cheese.

Line 8 muffin moulds with a disc of baking parchment then spoon in the mixture and smooth over or leave rustic. Brush the surface with milk and bake in the oven for about 35–40 minutes. To test if ready, take one out and tap the base, which should sound hollow. Turn out onto racks to cool.

That taco moment

Per serving

156 cals   2.3g fibre
5.8g fat   0.9g salt
2.4g saturates
4.5g sugar   **2.5g fat per 100g**

A young snack I know, but it's good to have youthful moments, and these are simple and tasty. Usually served with beef mince, I've reduced the fat by using turkey.

Makes 8

spray of olive oil

2 garlic cloves, crushed to a paste with a little salt

1 small onion, finely chopped

200g turkey mince

1 teaspoon chilli powder

½ teaspoon ground cumin

½ teaspoon ground coriander

2 x 300g tin red kidney beans, drained and rinsed

2 tablespoons tomato purée

300ml chicken stock

1 x 200g tin chopped tomatoes

8 taco shells

½ small iceberg lettuce, shredded finely

SALSA:

½ cucumber, deseeded and finely sliced

1 small red onion, finely diced

2 tomatoes, deseeded and diced

1 tablespoon chopped coriander

juice of 2 limes

2 teaspoons sweet chilli sauce

Preheat the oven to 160°C/gas mark 2.

Spray a little oil into a frying pan and cook the garlic, onion and turkey mince until golden brown, breaking up any lumps with a wooden spoon.

Add the chilli powder, cumin, ground coriander, kidney beans, tomato purée and stock and bring to the boil. Reduce the heat and simmer for 20 minutes, until the liquid reduces considerably. Fold in the tomatoes and season.

Meanwhile, make the salsa by combining all the ingredients and warm the taco shells in the oven for 6–7 minutes.

Place the taco shells, turkey mixture, lettuce and salsa on the table for your diners to assemble themselves.

Tip

A dollop of 0% fat Greek yogurt on top of each taco gives a creamy, cooling effect.

Honey-glazed chicken drumsticks

Per serving	
182 cals	1.2g fibre
5.2g fat	0.9g salt
1g saturates	
11.8g sugar	**2.4g fat per 100g**

This is one to have ready for when you have those hunger pangs. The steamed drumsticks can be prepared in advance and then simply tossed with the other ingredients when you fancy a nibble. They can be eaten hot or cold.

Serves 4

8 skinless chicken drumsticks
2 teaspoons vegetable oil
1 onion, cut into 8 wedges
3 tomatoes, roughly chopped
2 tablespoons runny honey
½ teaspoon garlic salt
½ teaspoon chilli powder
2 teaspoons curry paste (hot or mild...
    your choice)

Using a Chinese bamboo steamer set over a wok, or an electric tiered steamer, steam the drumsticks for 20 minutes.

Heat the oil in a wok or frying pan, then add the onion wedges and cook over a medium heat for 12–15 minutes, then add the tomatoes honey, garlic salt, chilli powder and curry paste. Stir to combine then cook gently for 3 minutes to blend all the ingredients.

Add the drumsticks and cook, turning continuously, for 4–5 minutes (if the drumsticks are hot from the steamer), until you build up a shiny glaze.

Tip

If glazing the chicken from cold, add a little water to the honey mixture to stop it burning and cook the chicken for 15 minutes. As the chicken heats up, the water will evaporate, leaving the honey glaze intact.

Prosciutto and nectarine skewers

Per serving	
92 cals	1.1g fibre
2.3g fat	0.9g salt
0.7g saturates	
13.2g sugar	**2g fat per 100g**

This is a yummy little snack that takes no time to knock together. If you're having friends over, make a few more and serve with drinks. They taste nice with a leaf salad, too.

Serves 4

4 slices prosciutto (Parma or
    Serrano ham)
4 nectarines, quartered and stones
    removed
1 tablespoon soft dark brown sugar
¼ teaspoon ground allspice
16 mint leaves

Lay the prosciutto slices on your work surface and cut each lengthways into four. Arrange the nectarine quarters, sideways on, at one end of each sliver of ham.

Combine the sugar with the allspice and sprinkle a little over the nectarine slices. Top each slice with a mint leaf, then roll up in the ham. Thread four slices onto a skewer (pre-soaked if wooden) and place under a hot grill, turning from time to time until the prosciutto is crisp.

Serve hot but warn your fellow diners.

Per serving

57 cals	1.9g fibre
2.1g fat	0.9g salt
0.4g saturates	
6.6g sugar	**1.1g fat per 100g**

Per serving

31 cals	1.5g fibre
0.2g fat	0.8g salt
0.1g saturates	
6.6g sugar	**0.2g fat per 100g**

Per serving

24 cals	0.8g fibre
0.3g fat	0.4g salt
0g saturates	
4.9g sugar	**0.5g fat per 100g**

Three simple salsas

Three flavour-filled salsas to accompany plain-cooked food, whether it's fish, chicken, pork or beef.

SWEET RED SALSA:

Serves 4

4 roasted red peppers from a jar, drained and roughly chopped
½ red onion, finely diced
3 ripe tomatoes, deseeded and diced
1 red chilli, deseeded and finely sliced
2 garlic cloves, crushed to a paste with a little salt
⅛ teaspoon sweet paprika
2 teaspoons rose harissa
2 teaspoons extra virgin olive oil
1 teaspoon red wine vinegar

Combine all the ingredients, check the seasoning and serve at room temperature.

ASIAN CRUNCH SALSA:

Serves 4

¼ cucumber, peeled, deseeded and finely diced
4 spring onions, thinly sliced
1 mango, peeled, stoned and finely diced
6 radishes, roughly diced
1 red chilli, deseeded and finely diced
2 bamboo shoots, finely diced
½ teaspoon grated ginger
grated zest and juice of 1 lime
1 tablespoon kecap manis
½ teaspoon nam pla (fish sauce)
2 teaspoons chopped mint

Combine all the ingredients, check the seasoning and serve chilled.

JAMAICAN CHILLI FIRE:

Serves 4

¼ pineapple, peeled, cored and diced
½ red pepper, deseeded and diced
3 spring onions, finely sliced
½ teaspoon chopped thyme
1 hot chilli, deseeded and finely diced
½ teaspoon ground cinnamon
1 garlic clove, crushed to a paste with a little salt
1 teaspoon sweet chilli sauce
2 teaspoons chopped coriander
½ teaspoon shop-bought jerk paste

Combine all the ingredients, check the seasoning and serve chilled.

Chinese pork in lettuce leaves

Per serving

195 cals
6.1g fat
2.1g saturates
3.4g sugar

1.1g fibre
2.4g salt

2.8g fat per 100g

This recipe is dedicated to my children, who love to eat it at our local Chinese – very moreish food that's ready in an instant and has smack-in-the-mouth flavours.

Serves 4

1 teaspoon sesame oil
1 small onion, finely chopped
1 teaspoon garlic paste
1 teaspoon ginger paste
1 medium red chilli, finely diced
325g extra lean pork mince
2 tablespoons mirin
85g button mushrooms, finely chopped
2 tablespoons kecap manis
2 tablespoons oyster sauce
juice of 1 lime
55g beansprouts
4 spring onions, finely sliced
1 teaspoon chopped mint
1 tablespoon chopped coriander
12 iceberg lettuce leaves

Heat the sesame oil in a wok, then add the onion, garlic, ginger and chilli and stir in briskly for 3 minutes. Add the pork, break up any lumps with the back of a spoon and cook until just brown.

Add the mirin, mushrooms, kecap manis, oyster sauce and lime juice and stir to try to combine. Quickly fold in the beansprouts, spring onions and herbs, and check the seasoning.

Serve with lettuce leaves, for your fellow diners to create their own lettuce wraps.

A neat little salad with colour

Per serving

121 cals
4g fat
0.8g saturates
9.2g sugar

2.3g fibre
0.8g salt

2.5g fat per 100g

Anything brightly coloured that jumps off the plate appears to taste better and loads of colour is excellent for different health benefits. This salad is knocked up in a flash and it has excellent results.

Serves 4

juice of 2 limes and grated zest of 1 lime
2 teaspoons nam pla (fish sauce)
1 teaspoon caster sugar
1 medium-size ripe but firm mango, peeled and roughly chopped
1 medium red onion, finely sliced
½ avocado peeled and cut into ½cm pieces
4 cherry tomatoes, halved
1 medium-heat green chilli, deseeded and finely diced
6 mint leaves, roughly chopped
½ small bunch of coriander, leaves only
200g tin of tuna in spring water, drained and flaked

Combine the lime juice, zest, nam pla and sugar in a bowl and stir until the sugar has dissolved.

In a separate bowl, combine the mango, onion, avocado, tomatoes and chilli. Pour over enough dressing to coat, dress on four plates then scatter with mint, coriander and tuna flakes.

Vegetarian rice-paper rolls

Per serving

39 cals   0.6g fibre

0.2g fat   0.7g salt

0g saturates

2.8g sugar   **0.5g fat per 100g**

These are all about crunch, texture and flavour. They make a lovely snack or something to serve with drinks, and the possible fillings are numerous and not just vegetarian – shreds of cooked chicken, salmon or prawns would all work well.

Makes 12

1 red pepper, deseeded and cut into
  julienne (thin strips)
1 small tin sliced bamboo shoots, cut
  into julienne
4 tinned palm hearts, cut into julienne
55g beansprouts
12 mint leaves, shredded
½ bunch of coriander, roughly chopped
12 rice-paper squares (24 x 17cm)

SAUCE:

2 garlic cloves, crushed to a paste
  with a little salt
1 tablespoon nam pla (fish sauce)
juice of 2 limes
2 tablespoons oyster sauce
3 teaspoons runny honey
2 teaspoons hot chilli sauce

Combine the first six ingredients in a bowl. In a separate bowl combine all the ingredients for the sauce.

Pour some warm water into another bowl and, working one at a time, dip a rice paper square into the water to soften, then place it on your work surface and pat it dry with kitchen paper..

To make up the roll, place the rice paper in front of you, in a diamond position, then arrange a small amount of the filling across the paper, with some sticking out at one end. Drizzle the vegetables with a little sauce, then roll up, tucking in one end but leaving one end open. Repeat with the remaining rice paper squares.

Light lunches and suppers

Basic pizza dough

Per serving

450 cals   4g fibre

2g fat   1.3g salt

0.3g saturates

2.6g sugar   **1g fat per 100g**

This is a staple recipe that will be useful for all sorts of toppings that can be low in fat. We normally associate cheese with pizza but there are some delicious toppings that can avoid the high fat content.

Makes 4 bases

7g fresh yeast, or 1 teaspoon dried

½ teaspoon caster sugar

500g plain flour, plus extra for dusting

380ml lukewarm water

1 teaspoon salt

spray of olive oil

For your starter dough, dissolve the yeast with the sugar plus 2 tablespoons of the flour in 50ml of the warm water. Leave for 5 minutes until it starts bubbling, then add the remaining water.

Add the salt and half the remaining flour and stir with your hand to form a paste. Gradually add the remaining flour until you have pliable dough. Shape into a ball and put in a bowl that you've sprayed with a little olive oil. Cover with clingfilm and leave in a warm place for 10 minutes.

Tip the dough onto a floured surface and knead with the heel of your hand for about 10 minutes until springy, smooth and elastic. Cut the dough into four equal parts, roll into balls and place on a lightly oil-sprayed flat tray, keeping each ball well apart. Cover with a damp tea-towel and leave in a warm place for 1 hour to rise.

A good tip for shaping the pizza base is to use the metal base of a loose-bottomed 23cm cake or tart tin. Push down the dough onto the well-floured tin and, with your fingertips, spread the dough until it fills the base, leaving the edge slightly thicker. You can then place the pizza base onto a flat, floured tray before arranging or spooning on a topping.

Basic tomato, oregano and garlic topping

Per serving
(including pizza base)
499 cals   4.4g fibre
4.7g fat   3g salt
0.7g saturates
5.1g sugar   **1.8g fat per 100g**

This is the simplest of toppings that you can add to or alter, for example by substituting basil for the oregano. Don't be tempted to use fresh oregano as the dried has a more genuine pizza taste and won't go black when cooked. Tomatoes are a great source of vitamin K and also include lycopene, which is an excellent antioxidant.

Makes 4 toppings

210ml passata
½ teaspoon dried oregano
¼ teaspoon dried chilli flakes
3 garlic cloves, crushed to a paste
  with a little sea salt
½ teaspoon freshly ground
  black pepper
8 anchovy fillets, rinsed, dried and
  cut in half lengthways
16 pitted Kalamata olives in brine,
  rinsed and halved
1 teaspoon extra virgin olive oil
1 quantity of Basic Pizza Dough (see
  page 93)

Preheat the oven to 240°C/gas mark 9, then place a flat roasting or Swiss roll tin in the oven to become extremely hot.

Meanwhile, make the topping sauce by combining the first five ingredients.

Remove the hot tray from the oven, flour the tray well and put on one or two bases, depending on their size. Spoon 2–3 tablespoons of the tomato sauce over the pizza base, leaving a 1cm border.

Arrange the slices of anchovy over the tomato sauce, then scatter each pizza with eight olive halves. Brush the border with a thick coating of olive oil.

Bake in the preheated oven for 8 minutes until crisp. Serve with a leaf salad.

Tip

Unless you have two large roasting tins, you may have to cook the pizzas individually or in two hits. And if you wish, you could use pickled anchovies instead of the ones preserved in oil.

Mini carrot 'cakes' with dried fruit

Per serving	
201 cals	7.3g fibre
1.6g fat	0.6g salt
0.3g saturates	
26.5g sugar	**0.5g fat per 100g**

These cakes-cum-burgers have been a favourite of mine for many a year. They have loads of flavour, with a lovely sweetness, and can be served as a vegetable side dish or as a light lunch served with salad.

Serves 4

10 medium carrots, cooked until soft and drained
6 tablespoons white breadcrumbs
6 dried apricots, finely diced
2 teaspoons chopped sultanas
4 spring onions, finely diced
4 garlic cloves, finely chopped
1 teaspoon chilli flakes
2 teaspoons grated orange rind
1 egg white
6 tablespoons mixed chopped parsley, mint and dill
flour, for coating
spray of vegetable oil, for frying
1 red onion, finely sliced
coriander leaves

Mash the carrots, then add the remaining ingredients up to the flour, and season. Knead the mixture well; if it's too wet, add further breadcrumbs – the mixture should be soft and slightly damp.

Mould the purée into four 'burgers' roughly 5cm across, coating your hands with flour to stop the mixture sticking.

Coat each cake in flour, then spray a non-stick frying pan with oil and cook the cakes gently until brown on both sides.

Serve with the finely sliced red onion and coriander leaves, as well as the yogurt dip described below.

Tip

Make sure the cooked carrots are really dry before mashing.

Herbed yogurt dip

Per serving	
27 cals	0g fibre
0g fat	0.1g salt
0g saturates	
2g sugar	**0g fat per 100g**

This dip is based on an Indian raita and goes really well with these carrot cakes and plain grilled fish.

Serves 4

200g 0% fat Greek yogurt
1 garlic clove, finely chopped
1 tablespoon chopped coriander
2 teaspoons chopped mint
¼ teaspoon ground black pepper

Combine all the ingredients together in a large bowl. Leave the flavours to develop for 1 hour before serving.

Season with salt just before eating.

Prawn tabbouleh jacket potatoes

Per serving
254 cals | 3.6g fibre
3.8g fat | 0.4g salt
0.5g saturates
3.3g sugar | **1.3g fat per 100g**

Made correctly, tabbouleh is a wonderful dish; it's when it's all grain and no green that it becomes a let-down. I've tried it here with jacket potatoes, which are a great source of carbohydrate and fibre, and their hot fluffiness prove an excellent marriage for the greens.

Serves 4

4 medium baking potatoes, washed
55g bulgar (cracked) wheat
55g flat-leaf parsley, leaves only,
   finely chopped
½ bunch of mint, leaves only, chopped
3 spring onions, thinly sliced
1 tomato, deseeded and diced
½ teaspoon ground cumin
1 tablespoon extra virgin olive oil
juice and grated zest of 1 unwaxed lemon
55g cooked North Atlantic prawns
2 tablespoons 0% fat yogurt
pinch of smoked paprika

Preheat the oven to 220°C/gas mark 7.

Place the potatoes on a rack over a roasting tray in the oven. Cook for 20 minutes then reduce the heat to 180°C/gas mark 4 and cook for a further 50 minutes.

Meanwhile, soak the bulgar wheat in cold water for 12–15 minutes, then drain and squeeze dry. Put in a bowl with the remaining ingredients except the yogurt and paprika. Mix to combine and season well.

Cut a large cross in the top of each potato, squeeze the sides to open the cross and top with the tabbouleh. Serve any extra on the side. Top with a dollop of yogurt and a sprinkling of paprika.

Tip

This may seem like a long cooking time for the potato but I like my centres really fluffy and the skins really crispy.

Per serving
(based on 24)
12 cals | 0.2g fibre
0.1g fat | 0.3g salt
0g saturates
1.2g sugar | **0.5g fat per 100g**

Cold oysters with spicy apple salsa

This salsa also works with cooked oysters, cooked mussels and grilled fish.

Makes 24

24 oysters, opened on the half shell
2 teaspoons runny honey
1 tablespoon nam pla (fish sauce)
juice of 2 limes and the grated zest of 1
1 hot red chilli, deseeded and finely diced
½ cucumber, peeled, deseeded and finely diced
1 Granny Smith apple, peeled and diced
2 spring onions, finely chopped
15 mint leaves, finely chopped

Place the oysters on a bed of ice.

Combine the remaining ingredients, check the seasoning, then spoon over the oysters half an hour before eating.

White bean, prawn and rocket salad

Per serving

130 cals   3.6g fibre

3.7g fat   0.9g salt

0.7g saturates

4.3g sugar   **1.9g fat per 100g**

Beans are a great source of fibre, and this salad mixes protein with carbs to help fill you up. A very quick salad to produce, this makes a lovely light lunch, served with warm, seeded bread.

Serves 4

1 x 400g tin cannellini beans, drained

1 tablespoon extra virgin olive oil

juice and zest of 1 unwaxed lemon

1 teaspoon runny honey

½ teaspoon black pepper

1 mild long red chilli, deseeded and finely chopped

1 garlic clove, crushed to a paste with a little salt

1 red onion, thinly sliced

1 stick celery, thinly sliced

6 button mushrooms, thinly sliced

16 cooked jumbo prawns, peeled

2 handfuls of rocket leaves

Heat the beans with a little salted water for 3 minutes, drain, then tip into a bowl. While still warm, combine the beans with the olive oil, lemon juice and zest, honey, pepper and chilli. Allow to cool, then combine with the remaining ingredients.

Tip

Feel free to change the beans to flageolet, borlotti or kidney, the prawns to cooked skinless chicken, and the rocket to watercress or chicory.

Teriyaki beef and mango kebabs

Per serving

499 cals   1.4g fibre

10.2g fat   3.1g salt

3.7g saturates

6.8g sugar   **2.7g fat per 100g**

The sweetness of this teriyaki marinade always goes down a treat. Serve with salad, rice or green vegetables.

Serves 4

450g sirloin steaks, fat removed

1 mango cut into 2cm chunks

4 spring onions, each cut into 2cm pieces

spray of vegetable oil

800g cooked rice, to serve

FOR THE MARINADE:

2 teaspoons cornflour

3 tablespoons sake or dry sherry

2 tablespoons rice vinegar

4 tablespoons kecap manis

2 garlic cloves, crushed to a paste with a little salt

½ teaspoon grated ginger

First start by making the marinade. Stir everything together and tip into a shallow dish.

Beat the steaks until very thin and cut into strips, then place in the marinade and leave for at least 2 hours.

Thread four pieces of each (beef, mango and spring onion) alternately on four, pre-soaked wooden skewers. The best way to place the steak on the skewers is to weave the strips concertina-style.

Heat the marinade in a small saucepan until hot, stirring from time to time.

Spray a large frying pan with vegetable oil until smoking, then place the skewers in the pan and cook for 1–3 minutes each side depending on how rare you like your meat. While the kebabs are cooking, baste regularly with the sauce.

A green tortilla

Per serving
(based on 4 servings)
294 cals   5.6g fibre
8.7g fat   1.2g salt
2.2g saturates
4.6g sugar   **2.8g fat per 100g**

Tortilla, frittata, Spanish omelette, what's in a name? All are variations on the same theme, though of course Spanish omelette IS a tortilla. This slow-cooked, deep-set omelette is delicious served at room temperature with a hunk of bread and a salad. Lots of protein, with a smattering of iron, vitamin A and a healthy dose of fibre, all go to make you feel really worthy. A great one for your lunchbox.

Serves 4–6

2 teaspoons olive oil
4 spring onions, finely sliced
1 courgette, cut into 1cm dice
85g frozen baby broad beans, defrosted
85g frozen peas, defrosted
150g cooked new potatoes, sliced
3 whole free-range eggs
3 egg whites
4 basil leaves, shredded

TO SERVE:

mixed salad leaves
4 thick slices of warm, crusty granary bread

Heat the oil in a 23cm non-stick, curved-sided frying pan until really smoking. Add the spring onions and courgette and cook over a medium heat for 6–8 minutes. Tip into a bowl and set aside.

Meanwhile, heat a small pan of salted water to boiling then add the broad beans and cook for 3 minutes. Drain, refresh and remove the leathery outer skin to reveal the emerald jewel-coloured vegetables. Combine these with the peas and new potatoes and add to the onions and courgettes.

Beat the whole eggs with the egg whites and fold into the vegetables. Add the basil and season.

Turn your grill on to high. Heat the curved-sided frying pan over a low heat, then tip in the omelette mixture and flatten gently to submerge the vegetables. Cook over a low heat for 8–10 minutes, then place under a hot grill for about 2 minutes, allowing the omelette to cook slightly before decanting it onto a flat plate.

Serve the tortilla while still slightly warm or at room temperature with the mixed salad and warm crusty bread.

Grilled polenta with wild mushrooms, bacon and thyme

Per serving	
278 cals	0.9g fibre
6g fat	3.9g salt
1.4g saturates	
1.3g sugar	**1.6g fat per 100g**

When did you last eat grilled polenta? It was fashionable for a few years then disappeared, which was a pity because it makes a great base for so many toppings, and for those with gluten intolerances it makes a good substitute for bruschetta. Tastes good with a dollop of fat-free Greek yogurt.

Serves 4

900ml vegetable or chicken stock
225g instant dried polenta
spray of olive oil
1 tablespoon olive oil
55g lean back bacon, fat and rind
    removed, cut into lardons
2 shallots, finely chopped
4 sprigs of thyme
3 garlic cloves, peeled and mashed to
    a paste with a little sea salt
225g mixed wild mushrooms (I like
    ceps, girolles and shiitakes), sliced
    if large
1 tablespoon snipped chives

Bring the stock to the boil, then pour in the polenta in a slow, steady trickle while you stir vigorously with a wooden spoon. Cook over a medium heat until the polenta starts to come away from the sides of the saucepan, about 5 minutes. Season generously.

Pour the polenta onto a lightly oil-sprayed, non-stick, shallow roasting tray, and spread it with the back of a wet spoon or palette knife until smooth and about 2.5cm thick. Leave to cool and thicken.

When the polenta has cooled, cut it into rectangles. (You may have more polenta than you need, but the leftovers can be cut into croûtons for soup.) Lightly spray a non-stick griddle pan with oil and cook over a medium heat until very hot. Cook the polenta rectangles until nicely marked on both sides, about 4 minutes.

Meanwhile, heat the olive oil in a non-stick frying pan, add the bacon and cook for 3 minutes. Add the shallots, thyme and garlic and stir to combine.

Increase the heat and stir in the mushrooms, then fry fiercely for about 2 minutes, stirring continuously. Season, then add the chives and spoon on top of the grilled polenta. Serve very hot.

Tip

Got a problem finding wild mushrooms? Never fear, just buy field or oyster mushrooms, slice them up and cook in the same way.

Thai fishcakes with cucumber dipping sauce

Per serving

242 cals	0.9g fibre
3.8g fat	2.9g salt
0.5g saturates	
18.3g sugar	**1g fat per 100g**

These fishcakes have a much tighter texture than your average British potato-based cakes, and because of this you should use only white filleted fish. Out of choice, I go for red snapper, which is really meaty and blends to a smooth paste. The fishcakes go well with a warm, crunchy salad.

Serves 4

500g red snapper fillets, cut into 2.5cm pieces

2 tablespoons red curry paste

3 fresh kaffir lime leaves, central spine removed

3 spring onions, finely sliced

1cm piece of root ginger, peeled and grated

1 egg white

1 tablespoon nam pla (fish sauce)

juice and zest of 1 lime

3 tablespoons coriander leaves, roughly chopped

40g extra fine beans, very finely sliced

55g corn kernels (tinned or frozen)

1 bird's eye chilli, deseeded and finely chopped

spray of vegetable oil

CUCUMBER DIPPING SAUCE:

½ cucumber, deseeded and cut into 5mm dice

½ teaspoon salt

55g caster sugar

120ml mirin

120ml water

120ml rice vinegar

½ tablespoon grated ginger root

1 tablespoon nam pla (fish sauce)

2 bird's eye chillies, finely chopped

2 spring onions, finely sliced

2 tablespoons chopped coriander

1 tablespoon chopped mint

For the dipping sauce, sprinkle the cucumber with a little salt in a sieve or colander and toss to combine, then leave for 20 minutes before rinsing.

Heat the sugar, mirin, water, vinegar and ginger in a saucepan, and stir until the sugar dissolves. Cool, then pour over the cucumber in the bowl. Fold in the remaining ingredients then refrigerate until ready to use.

For the fishcakes, put the fish, curry paste, lime leaves, spring onions, ginger, egg white, nam pla, lime juice and zest into a food-processor and blend until smooth. Spoon into a bowl, then fold in the remaining ingredients except the oil.

With wet hands, roll the fish paste into small balls then flatten into smooth cakes. You should produce about 16 fishcakes altogether.

Spray the cakes top and bottom with the oil. Heat a large frying pan, preferably non-stick, and cook the fishcakes in batches for 3 minutes on each side until golden. Keep warm in a low oven while you cook the rest.

Serve with the cucumber dipping sauce.

Tip

If you can't find red snapper, pollack works well, is sustainable and good value.

Baked sweet potato with sea bass ceviche

Per serving

334 cals   6.8g fibre

3.9g fat   0.4g salt

0.7g saturates

19.7g sugar   **0.7g fat per 100g**

A cracking dish for summer or winter, with contrasting textures and temperatures. The lime juice 'cooks' the sea bass by marination, the longer you leave it in the marinade the more it will cook. If you're a fan of sashimi, dress the fish just before serving.

Serves 2

2 sweet potatoes (approx. 400g), halved and washed, skin on

1 medium-heat chilli, deseeded and very thinly sliced

½ red onion, very finely sliced

6 radishes, topped and tailed and very thinly sliced

1 large, vine-ripened tomato, deseeded and cut into small dice

½ cucumber, deseeded and cut into small dice

juice of 2 limes

2 teaspoons rapeseed oil

1 teaspoon caster sugar

225g skinless sea bass fillet

½ bunch of coriander, leaves and stems roughly chopped

Preheat the oven to 200°C/gas mark 6.

Place the potato halves on the rack in the oven and cook for 40 minutes or until tender.

In a bowl or dish, combine the chilli, red onion, radishes, diced tomato and cucumber, lime juice, oil and sugar. Leave for 15 minutes, stirring from time to time.

Depending on how you like your fish 'cooked', cut the sea bass into thin strips or thicker batons and place in the marinade about 15 minutes before serving.

When the sweet potato is cooked, remove from the oven and leave to cool a little. Once cool enough to handle, thinly slice each half in the skin and arrange on two plates. Scatter over the ceviche and top off with coriander.

Tip

You can try all sorts of fish here – scallops, prawns, salmon, tuna and swordfish, for instance – and a teensy-weensy amount of diced avocado adds colour and tastes great, too.

Crab and corncakes, soy dip

Per serving

184 cals   1.1g fibre

1.6g fat   3.7g salt

0.2g saturates

7.3g sugar   **0.8g fat per 100g**

Crab cakes are always a popular choice at my Greyhound pub near Henley-on-Thames. Here, I've given the cakes more texture by adding celery, red pepper and sweetcorn. Crab is a good source of zinc and iron, and the addition of vegetables will give this dish some fibre, too. A cucumber salad to go with the cakes would add even more fibre.

Serves 4

CRAB CAKES:

spray of vegetable oil

3 spring onions, finely chopped

1 stalk celery, finely diced

½ red pepper, deseeded and cut into long thin strips, then diced

2 tablespoons frozen or drained tinned sweetcorn

325g fresh or drained tinned white crabmeat

2 egg whites, beaten

1 tablespoon chopped coriander

1 tablespoon reduced-salt soy sauce

70g dry white breadcrumbs

SOY DIP:

60ml reduced-salt soy sauce

1 spring onion, finely chopped

2 teaspoons finely chopped coriander

1 teaspoon finely chopped mint

1 red bird's eye chilli, very finely diced

1 tablespoon mirin (optional)

½ tablespoon runny honey

For the dip, combine all the ingredients and leave for at least 1 hour to allow the flavours to develop.

For the crab cakes, spray a frying pan with a light coating of oil, then, over a medium heat, cook the spring onions, celery and pepper for 8–10 minutes, until the vegetables have started to soften. Allow to cool in a bowl.

When the vegetables have cooled, fold in the remaining ingredients and mix well, using your hands. Shape into four large or eight smaller crab cakes, place in your refrigerator and ideally leave for a couple of hours to dry out and firm up.

Spray a little oil in a frying pan and cook the crab cakes over a medium heat for 2–3 minutes each side, until golden. Serve with the soy dip.

Tip

Even better, leave the crab cakes covered in your refrigerator overnight before cooking so they firm up even more.

Crab, rocket and chilli pasta

Per serving
(using canned crab)

301 cals	2.5g fibre
4.7g fat	1.5g salt
0.7g saturates	
1.2g sugar	**1.5g fat per 100g**

Instant pleasure, so simple and yet really zingy. Fresh crabmeat is preferable but tinned is far superior to frozen, if fresh is unavailable. This will take you no time at all, I would rather wait the 10 minutes for dried pasta to cook then shortening the time by using fresh pasta, and as a bonus, crab contains a decent whack of omega-3 fats. .

Serves 4

2 large or medium red chillies, finely sliced

2 garlic cloves, crushed to a paste with a
  little Maldon salt

grated zest and juice of 1 unwaxed lemon

1 tablespoon extra virgin olive oil

350g fresh or canned white crabmeat

225g dried linguine or spaghetti

3 tablespoons rough chopped parsley

2 handfuls of washed rockets leaves

Add the chilli, garlic, lemon zest and juice and olive oil to the crabmeat and mix to combine. Season to taste.

Heat a large pan of salted water until boiling, then add the pasta and stir until you're sure the pasta will not stick together. Cook until al dente, then drain and return to the pan with a little water still clinging to the pasta. Fold in the parsley and rocket and cook over a very low heat until the greens have wilted.

Fold in the crab mix, cook for a further 1 minute, then serve immediately in warm bowls.

Mediterranean vegetable pasta

Per serving

397 cals	7.4g fibre
5.5g fat	1g salt
0.8g saturates	
11.8g sugar	**0.9g fat per 100g**

When you've got all these exciting flavours, there's no need for meat or fish to come into the equation.

Serves 4

1 tablespoon olive oil

1 red onion, finely chopped

3 garlic cloves, finely chopped

25g dry-pack sun-dried tomatoes, chopped

4 canned artichokes, drained and chopped

115g roasted red peppers from a jar,
  chopped

1 aubergine, finely diced

1 courgette, finely diced

1 x 400g tin cherry tomatoes

325g dried penne

6 basil leaves, shredded

In a large saucepan, heat the olive oil, then add the onion and garlic and cook slowly for 10 minutes before adding all the remaining vegetables except for the tinned tomatoes. Toss to combine and cook for 3 minutes.

Add the tinned tomatoes and cook gently for 15 minutes until thickening, then season well.

Meanwhile, cook the penne in boiling salted water, according to the manufacturer's instructions or until al dente. Drain in a colander and, with the water still dripping, add to the sauce. Stir to combine, fold in the basil and serve immediately with salad and bread.

Vegetable paella

Per serving

449 cals	5.9g fibre
8.5g fat	3.7g salt
2g saturates	
8.5g sugar	**1.5g fat per 100g**

Whether you're a vegetarian or not, this dish, rich in earth flavours, will suit most tastes. Unlike with risotto, you don't have to stand over the pan stirring continuously.

Serves 4

900ml vegetable stock
200ml water
1 tablespoon olive oil
1 large onion, finely chopped
3 garlic cloves, finely chopped
2 bay leaves
2 sprigs of thyme
2 dried chillies
1 red pepper, deseeded and
    finely chopped
pinch of saffron stamens
½ teaspoon ground turmeric
2 teaspoons sweet paprika
325g Calasparra or Arborio rice
115g frozen petits pois, defrosted
115g frozen baby broad beans,
    defrosted
1 large courgette, cut into 5mm dice
12 pitted black olives, in brine
2 tablespoons chopped parsley

Heat the stock and water in a pan to boiling.

Meanwhile, in a large frying pan, heat the oil then cook the onion, garlic, bay leaves, thyme and chillies gently for 10–12 minutes, until soft but not brown. Stir in the red pepper, saffron, turmeric, paprika and rice until well combined. Cook for 2 minutes.

Add the stock and water, bring to the boil, then reduce the heat and cook for approximately 18 minutes, until the liquid has evaporated. Stir in the peas, broad beans, courgette and olives, cover with a lid, turn off the heat and leave for 5 minutes.

Season, give it a good stir, then sprinkle with the chopped parsley and serve.

Prawn tortillas with mango salad

Per serving

422 cals   5.9g fibre

2.3g fat   2g salt

0.3g saturates

18.9g sugar   **0.5g fat per 100g**

These tortillas are quick and easy to make; they're low in fat and high in fibre with the added bonus of two full-on antioxidants – beta-carotene and vitamin C. More importantly, they are delicious.

Serves 4

spray of olive oil

40 raw tiger prawns, shell off, tail on,
   deveined

2 garlic cloves, finely chopped

1 red chilli, deseeded and finely sliced

8 flour tortillas

coriander sprigs and lime wedges,
   to serve

MANGO SALAD:

½ red onion, finely sliced

3 spring onions, finely sliced on
   the diagonal

2 ripe but firm mangoes, peeled,
   stoned and cut into 1cm dice

1 red chilli, deseeded and finely diced

8 cherry tomatoes, halved

½ cucumber, peeled, deseeded and
   cut into 1cm dice

6 radishes, finely sliced

1 tablespoon coriander leaves

1 teaspoon chopped mint

juice of 2 limes and zest of 1 lime

1 tablespoon nam pla (fish sauce)

1 tablespoon liquid honey

For the mango salad, combine all the ingredients in a bowl, check the seasoning then refrigerate.

Preheat the oven to 160°C/gas mark 2.

Spray a griddle pan with oil, set the heat to high, then pan-fry the prawns for 1 minute on each side. Add the garlic and chilli and cook for a further 1 minute, tossing the prawns from time to time.

Meanwhile, wrap the tortillas in foil and place in the oven to warm through.

To serve, fold the tortillas in four and place two on each plate with 10 prawns on top, accompanied by the mango salad and some coriander sprigs and lime wedges. Get your guests to create their own wraps.

Asian chicken burgers

Per serving

383 cals   3.5g fibre

7.3g fat   2g salt

1.4g saturates

9.3g sugar   **2g fat per 100g**

We all love burgers, there's no denying it, and that's not such a bad thing. Here, I've reduced the fat by using chicken mince and added a little interest by using Asian ingredients.

Serves 4

450g chicken mince (if you can't get it
    use 225g each of light and dark meat,
    and mince it yourself in a processor)
85g fresh breadcrumbs
3 garlic cloves, crushed to a paste
    with a little salt
2 Thai red chillies, deseeded and
    finely chopped
½ bunch of coriander, finely chopped
1 tablespoon chopped mint
2 tablespoons sweet chilli sauce
1 tablespoon hot chilli oil
1 teaspoon ground coriander
4 spring onions, finely sliced
2 teaspoons nam pla (fish sauce)
spray of vegetable oil

TO SERVE:

4 onion buns, strips of carrot,
    cucumber shavings, coriander leaves,
    shaved red onion and tomato slices

Put all the ingredients for the burger in a clean bowl and mix well with wet hands. Divide the mixture into four then shape into burger patties. Ideally, refrigerate for 1 hour to allow them to firm up.

Spray a large frying pan with vegetable oil and cook the burgers for 4–5 minutes each side over a medium heat.

Serve on toasted buns garnished with salad ingredients.

Tip

A good dressing for the salad ingredients would be to mix together 2 teaspoons of caster sugar, the juice of 2 limes and 1 tablespoon of nam pla, stirred until the sugar dissolves.

Mussels in a Provençal sauce

Per serving
240 cals   1.5g fibre
7.4g fat   1.9g salt
1g saturates
6.2g sugar   **1.1g fat per 100g**

Mussels are probably the sweetest of all the shellfish and they are definitely the best value. Here, I've put them in a tomato sauce which should be served with crusty bread.

Serves 4

1 tablespoon olive oil
1 onion, finely chopped
3 garlic cloves, finely chopped
2 anchovy fillets, roughly chopped
1 teaspoon chopped thyme leaves
2 bay leaves
180ml dry white wine
1 x 400g tin chopped tomatoes
1 teaspoon caster sugar
2 slices of orange peel
2kg cleaned mussels
2 tablespoons chopped Kalamata olives

In a large saucepan, heat the olive oil then add the onion, garlic, anchovy fillets, thyme and bay. Cook gently for 10 minutes until the onions have softened.

Add the wine, bring to the boil and cook until most of the liquid has evaporated.

Add the tomatoes, sugar and orange peel and cook for 8 minutes before increasing the heat and adding the mussels. Cover with a lid and cook for 5 minutes, shaking the pan from time to time. Discard any mussels that don't open. Finally fold in the olives, check the seasoning and serve piping hot with salad and crusty bread.

Per serving
125 cals   1g fibre
1.7g fat   1.9g salt
0.3g saturates
0.7g sugar   **1.2g fat per 100g**

Spanish shrimp pancakes

In Spain, you'd get these pancakes made with shell-on shrimps, but I think we'd prefer not to eat head and shells. Peeled brown shrimps are becoming more widely available, but if you can't find them use cooked pink prawns which you can slice finely. Serve the pancakes with a yogurt dip and salad.

Serves 4

85g plain flour
1 teaspoon baking powder
½ teaspoon salt
½ teaspoon ground black pepper
½ teaspoon sweet paprika
¼ teaspoon chilli powder
4 tablespoons chopped parsley
4 spring onions, finely chopped
225g peeled brown shrimp
1 egg white, beaten to stiff peaks
spray of oil

Sift the flour, baking powder and salt in a bowl, then add the pepper, paprika, chilli powder, parsley and spring onions. Stir to combine then make a well in the centre and gradually add enough water to make a batter the consistency of double cream (up to 150ml water). Cover with clingfilm and set aside for 1 hour.

Fold in the shrimps, then the beaten egg whites.

Heat a large, non-stick frying pan, spray with oil, then drop in tablespoons of the batter and allow to spread out to about 2.5cm. Cook over a medium heat for about 2 minutes or until little bubbles appear on the surface. Flip over and cook for another minute until golden on both sides.

Steak sandwich with onion and mushroom relish

Per serving

378 cals	5.3g fibre
7.1g fat	1.5g salt
2.3g saturates	
19.8g sugar	**2g fat per 100g**

I had to find a way to get a steak sandwich into the recipe list and, while you don't automatically associate steak with a low-fat diet, I've reduced the meat weight and upped the vegetables, thereby achieving my aim.

Serves 4

spray of olive oil
4 x 60g fillet steaks, trimmed of any
  fat and beaten thin
8 slices of wholegrain bread
handful of baby spinach leaves
1 beefsteak tomato, sliced into 8

ONION AND MUSHROOM RELISH:

1 teaspoon olive oil
3 red onions, finely sliced
1 garlic clove, crushed to a paste with
  a little salt
2 tablespoons thyme leaves
½ teaspoon ground black pepper
225g button mushrooms, sliced
2 tablespoons soft brown sugar
2 tablespoons sherry vinegar

To make the onion and mushroom relish, heat the olive oil in a saucepan, add the onion, garlic, thyme and black pepper, cover with a circle of wet parchment paper and cover with a lid and cook over a very low heat for 45 minutes to 1 hour, stirring every 10 minutes or so. The onion will slowly collapse to a caramelised pile.

Discard the parchment paper, then increase the heat, add the mushrooms and stir to combine. Cook for a further 8 minutes, until the mushrooms have released their liquids. Add the brown sugar and vinegar and cook briefly to combine the flavours, then set aside to keep warm.

Spray the steaks with a little oil and season with salt and pepper, then cook on a hot griddle pan for 45 seconds to 1 minute on both sides.

Toast the bread, then place one slice on each of four plates, top with a loosely arranged pile of spinach, followed by 2 slices of tomato and some relish. Then place the steak on top, followed by a second slice of bread.

Rosemary lamb with beans and penne

This is one of those dishes that looks a bit of a jumble but the flavours gel – not everything is about looks. It also tastes great at room temperature.

Serves 4

300g pencil fillet of lamb, trimmed
    of visible fat
1 teaspoon olive oil
1 teaspoon ground black pepper
½ teaspoon Maldon salt
1 teaspoon very finely chopped
    rosemary
½ teaspoon ground cumin
1 teaspoon garlic paste
zest and juice of 1 unwaxed lemon
275g dried penne pasta
175g extra fine, crunchy French beans,
    topped, tailed and each bean cut
    into three
300ml tomato passata
1 x 400g flageolet beans, drained
    and rinsed
3 tomatoes, deseeded and diced
¼ bunch flat-leaf parsley, leaves
    picked

Preheat the oven to 180°C/gas mark 4.

Place the lamb in a dish and rub with olive oil. Combine the black pepper, salt, rosemary, cumin, garlic paste and lemon zest. Roll the lamb in this mixture, coating all sides of the meat, then leave for up to 2 hours.

Bring a large pan of salted water to the boil and cook the penne according to the manufacturer's instructions, keeping the pasta al dente. Drain and keep warm.

Cook the French beans in salted water for 4 minutes, then drain and refresh in cold water.

Heat an ovenproof frying pan and seal the lamb all over until golden. Do not cook over too high a heat, otherwise you'll scorch the spice coating, rendering it bitter. Place the pan in the oven and cook for 12 minutes, then remove and allow the lamb to rest in a warm place.

Deglaze the lamb pan with the passata and lemon juice and boil for 5 minutes. Add the penne, flageolet beans and green beans, toss to combine and heat through. Fold in the tomato and parsley leaves and cook until the parsley has wilted. Season well.

Spoon the pasta and beans into four warm bowls then thinly carve the lamb and arrange on top.

Poached pollack with fennel sauce

Per serving
402 cals 5.6g fibre
6.8g fat 0.9g salt
1.8g saturates
19.2g sugar **1g fat per 100g**

Pollack is a sustainable fish but personally I don't think it's a fish that stands alone; it needs a sauce. So this sauce encompasses the flavour of the fennel that goes well with the fish but it also includes all your vegetables.

Serves 4

750ml skimmed milk
1 bay leaf
pinch of grated nutmeg
2 carrots, peeled and cut into 1cm dice
1 head of fennel, outside layer
    removed then the remainder
    cut into 1cm dice
8 new potatoes, peeled or not,
    cut into 1cm dice
1 onion, finely sliced
4 x 175g fillets of pollack
40g low-fat spread
40g plain flour
115g frozen petits pois, defrosted
2 tomatoes, deseeded and diced
2 teaspoons chopped dill

Place the milk in a saucepan with the bay leaf, nutmeg, carrots, fennel, new potatoes and onion. Bring to the boil and simmer for 15–20 minutes to cook the vegetables.

Place the pollack in the milk and poach for 5 minutes, then remove and keep warm. Strain the milk, retaining both the milk and vegetables separately but discarding the bay leaf. Keep the milk hot.

Place the low-fat spread in a non-stick pan with the cooked vegetables. When the spread has melted and is bubbling, add the flour and stir to combine. Gradually add the cooked milk, stirring constantly. You will not need all the milk, you're looking for a sauce the thickness of double cream. But as it cooks, the sauce will thicken so keep adding the milk until the sauce no longer tastes floury, probably about 15 minutes. Season well. Finally, fold in the peas, tomatoes and dill.

Place the pollack in a presentable baking dish then pour over the hot sauce and place under the grill until the sauce and fish bubble gently. Serve piping hot.

Tip

The trick to a good béchamel-style sauce is to cook the roux (flour and fat) for a few minutes then cook the sauce for long enough to eliminate that floury taste.

Colour co-ordinated sweet potato

Per serving

225 cals   5.9g fibre

1.2g fat   0.3g salt

0.3g saturates

16.5g sugar   **0.4g fat per 100g**

Why don't we eat more sweet potatoes? They're yummy, with a natural sweetness and great colour. Treat them exactly as you would normal potatoes, though they cook a little quicker and they've got a better GI rating. With these baked potatoes, all you need is a salad.

Serves 4

4 medium sweet potatoes (approx. 720g), washed

½ red onion, sliced

2 spring onions, finely sliced

1 tablespoon roughly chopped coriander

¼ teaspoon ground cumin

½ teaspoon Tabasco

2 tablespoons 0% fat Greek yogurt

1 tablespoon sweet chilli sauce

juice of 1 lime

½ red pepper, finely diced

125g sweetcorn kernels, drained

55g frozen petits pois, defrosted

1 x 80g tin yellowfin tuna in spring water, drained

Preheat the oven to 200°C/gas mark 6.

Place the sweet potatoes on a rack set over a roasting tray and cook for approximately 40 minutes or until tender when pierced with a knife.

Meanwhile, combine the remaining ingredients in a bowl and leave for the flavours to develop while the potatoes are cooking. Season.

Cut the sweet potatoes three-quarters deep from end to end and prise open. Spoon a quarter of the mixture into each one.

Tip

Feel free to substitute prawns, tinned crab or tinned salmon for the tuna for a change, and the mixture also works well with shredded, cooked turkey or chicken.

A warm salad of pumpkin, mint and chilli

Per serving

63 cals	3g fibre
0.9g fat	1.5g salt
0.3g saturates	
9g sugar	**0.3g fat per 100g**

This is such a tasty vegetarian dish and nowadays I eat more and more of this style of food, reducing my meat intake and putting loads of flavour into delicious vegetables. Think of the pumpkin as an orange courgette, requiring very little cooking. In fact, the salad works very well with courgettes or butternut squash instead of the pumpkin, and with rocket added in place of the spinach.

Serves 4

1kg pumpkin, peeled, deseeded and thinly sliced in manageable pieces

3 garlic cloves, thinly sliced

3 Thai bird's eye chillies, thinly sliced

spray of vegetable oil

115g mangetout, topped and tailed and thinly sliced

4 spring onions, thinly sliced on the diagonal

60ml vegetable stock

3 tablespoons reduced-salt soy sauce

2.5cm piece of root ginger, peeled and cut into julienne (small batons)

2 teaspoons honey

12 mint leaves

2 handfuls of baby spinach, washed

Put the pumpkin, garlic and chilli in a bowl and spray with oil. Toss to combine then season with salt and pepper.

Heat a large saucepan, add the pumpkin mixture, then cover with a lid and cook for 6 minutes, shaking the pan from time to time.

Remove the lid, add the mangetout, spring onions, vegetable stock, soy sauce and ginger, and cook over a medium heat for 3 minutes. Finally, add the honey, mint and spinach and stir to combine. Cook until the spinach starts to wilt, about 1 minute.

Serve hot or at room temperature.

Flash-fried rice

Per serving

388 cals	3.4g fibre
8.8g fat	1.8g salt
2.3g saturates	
12.4g sugar	**2.4g fat per 100g**

I'm a bit of a fan of fried rice. It's just that the word 'fried' doesn't instill confidence for those on a low-fat diet. However, I've discovered a different method that produces a similar effect but doesn't need very much fat.

Serves 4

2 x 250g packs of 2-minute microwavable long-grain rice (see Tip)

spray of oil

4 spring onions, finely sliced

2 long green chillies, finely sliced

1 red pepper, deseeded and cut into thin strips

115g extra fine green beans, cut into 2.5cm pieces

55g frozen petits pois, defrosted

¼ Savoy cabbage, shredded and washed

325g skinless cooked chicken, diced

1 tablespoon soft dark brown sugar

½ chicken stock cube, crumbled

2 tablespoons reduced-salt soy sauce

2 tablespoons sweet chilli sauce

½ bunch of roughly chopped coriander

Preheat the oven to 200°C/gas mark 6.

Line a shallow roasting tray with non-stick parchment paper. Tip the rice onto the paper, breaking up any lumps, and spray the surface with oil. Place in the oven and cook for 12 minutes – it should be crispy on the surface. Season and set aside to keep warm.

Meanwhile, spray a wok (ideally non-stick) with a good coating of oil and, over a high heat, fry the spring onions, chillies, red pepper and beans for 2 minutes, stirring continuously.

Add the peas, cabbage and chicken and fry to give a little colour and to wilt the cabbage, about 3 minutes.

Sprinkle over the sugar and stock cube, then add the rice, breaking up any lumps. Stir-fry for 2 minutes, then add the remaining ingredients. Cook for 1 minute then serve very hot.

Tip

I know it's lazy, but I'm a supporter of quick-cook rice. If you feel you want to cook your own from scratch, feel free, but make sure that you cool it quickly after cooking and make sure that it is very dry and that the grains are separate – use kitchen paper, if necessary.

Tagliatelle with cumin-roasted cherry tomatoes

Per serving

317 cals   4.8g fibre

3.1g fat   0.3g salt

0.5g saturates

4.9g sugar   **0.8g fat per 100g**

A little pre-planning is required for this sweet pasta dish, but I think it's worth the effort. Sacrifice some time in the name of simplicity because the roasting process really intensifies the tomato flavour and increases the fibre content.

Serves 4

450g cherry tomatoes, halved

spray of olive oil

3 garlic cloves, very finely chopped

¼ teaspoon dried chilli flakes

2 teaspoons cumin seeds

1 teaspoon fennel seeds

325g dried tagliatelle

6 basil leaves, ripped

handful of baby spinach leaves

Preheat the oven to 140°C/gas mark 1–2.

Arrange the cherry tomatoes, cut side up, on a roasting tray lined with greaseproof paper. Spray the tomatoes with a mist of olive oil, then scatter with the chopped garlic and chilli flakes and sprinkle with the seeds. Place in the preheated oven for about 1 hour, or until the tomatoes have slightly shrivelled but not become too brown.

Towards the halfway stage of the tomatoes cooking, start thinking about the pasta by bringing a large pan of salted water to the boil. Add the pasta 10 minutes before the tomatoes are ready, stir for a couple of minutes, then cook until al dente – which is about 1 minute less than the manufacturer recommends.

Remove the tomatoes from the oven and tip them, with any juices, into a frying pan. Drain the pasta using a pasta ladle, then ladle onto the tomatoes with a little of the cooking water. Carefully place the basil and spinach on top of the pasta and then continue to toss or turn over the pasta until the spinach has wilted. You're bound to lose a few leaves to the hob top, so you may prefer to add the spinach little by little.

Season to taste and serve immediately.

Tip

You may be tempted to use sun-dried tomatoes in olive oil. *Don't!* It's cheating; they don't taste as good and in any case they're saturated in olive oil.

A simple vegetable curry

Per serving

150 cals   4.7g fibre

3g fat   1.3g salt

0.6g saturates

10.2g sugar   **0.7g fat per 100g**

You must not feel daunted by the idea of making curry at home – it's just a case of having a few spices in your cupboard. This curry can be easily adapted to suit different tastes. If you choose different vegetables, just make sure you add them at the right time; if using more root vegetables, for example, add them at the same time as the potatoes.

Serves 8

1 tablespoon vegetable oil

1 onion, roughly chopped

1 teaspoon grated ginger

4 garlic cloves, crushed to a paste with a little salt

½ teaspoon chilli powder

1 teaspoon ground cumin

1 teaspoon ground coriander

½ teaspoon ground fennel

3 cardamom pods, lightly crushed

½ teaspoon ground black pepper

1 teaspoon ground turmeric

8 new potatoes, halved

600ml vegetable stock

½ butternut squash, peeled, deseeded and cut into 2.5cm dice

½ cauliflower, broken into florets

2 courgettes, cut into 2.5cm rounds

3 tomatoes, roughly chopped

1 teaspoon garam masala

85g frozen petits pois, defrosted

2 medium-heat green chillies, deseeded and sliced

2 handfuls of baby spinach leaves

4 tablespoons 0% fat Greek yogurt

Heat the oil in a large saucepan, then cook the onion, ginger and garlic over a low heat for 10–12 minutes until the onion starts to soften. Add the spices, toss to combine, and cook for 1 minute.

Add the halved potatoes and cook until they start to stick slightly, then pour in the stock, bring to the boil and cook for 5 minutes. Add the butternut squash, cauliflower and courgettes and cook for 6 minutes.

Fold in the tomatoes, garam masala, peas, chillies and spinach, stir to combine and cook for 3 minutes. Check the seasoning and serve with rice and a dollop of yogurt.

A pot of spiced chicken livers

Per serving
250 cals
5.9g fat
0.9g saturates
9.5g sugar

4.7g fibre
1g salt

1.5g fat per 100g

Offal, apart from calf's liver, generally presents exceptional value, and chicken livers are also very nutritious. If you love your liver, like me, you'll really enjoy this quick, good-value dish. Serve with crusty bread.

Serves 4

450g chicken livers, trimmed
and cubed
4 tablespoons 0% fat Greek yogurt
½ teaspoon ground cumin
½ teaspoon ground coriander
½ teaspoon ground fennel
1 teaspoon ground turmeric
4 garlic cloves, mashed to a paste
with a little salt
2 onions, 1 roughly chopped,
1 finely sliced
1 teaspoon grated ginger
1 medium-heat chilli, deseeded
and roughly chopped
3 tablespoons shop-bought
tikka paste
½ bunch of coriander, roughly
chopped
spray of vegetable oil
1 x 400g tin chopped tomatoes
1 teaspoon rose harissa
1 x 400g tin of white beans, rinsed
and drained

Combine the chicken livers with the yogurt, cumin, coriander, fennel, turmeric and half the garlic, and leave to marinate while you cook the sauce.

Put the remaining garlic in a food-processor with the roughly chopped onion, ginger, chilli, tikka paste and coriander and blend to a smooth purée. Set aside.

Spray a saucepan with the vegetable oil, add the onion slices and cook over a medium heat for 5 minutes to soften them. Add the puréed onion paste, along with the chopped tomatoes, and bring to the boil. Reduce the heat and simmer for 15 minutes.

Meanwhile, scrape the yogurt off the livers and add this to the pan. Stir to combine.

Heat a frying pan with oil and, over a fierce heat, fry the chicken livers for 1 minute each side. Tip into the tomato sauce with the harissa and beans. Warm through and season.

Sea bass carpaccio with shaved vegetables

Per serving

114 cals   1.7g fibre
3.7g fat   0.2g salt
0.6g saturates
3.4g sugar   **1.8g fat per 100g**

I do like raw fish but it obviously has to be incredibly fresh. This recipe 'cooks' the sea bass by marination. Vegetable shavings look really cute on the plate and the crunch is in contrast to the soft texture of the sea bass.

Serves 4

1 small fennel bulb, outside layer removed, the remainder cut into paper-thin slivers
1 carrot, peeled and thinly shaved using a peeler
½ cucumber, peeled and shaved using a peeler (discard seeds)
4 radishes, very thinly sliced
1 teaspoon chopped mint
1 teaspoon chopped dill
1 teaspoon caster sugar
¼ teaspoon salt
¼ teaspoon ground white pepper
juice of 1 lemon
2 teaspoons extra virgin olive oil
325g sea bass fillets

In a bowl, combine the fennel, carrot, cucumber and radishes. Toss to combine.

In a separate bowl, combine the mint, dill, sugar, salt, pepper and lemon juice. Stir to combine then add the olive oil.

Slice the sea bass paper thin with a sharp knife (you should be able to see the knife through the sea bass) and arrange on four cold plates.

Scatter the vegetable ribbons over the sea bass, then drizzle the herb dressing over the vegetables. Leave for 20 minutes before serving.

Tip

This recipe works well with salmon, although the fat content will be higher, or you could try thinly sliced scallops, swordfish or raw oysters.

Spaghetti with red pepper and shellfish

Per serving

385 cal   4.1g fibre
4.3g fat   1.3g salt
0.7g saturates
3.9g sugar   **1g fat per 100g**

I usually avoid cooked seafood at the supermarket but occasionally, when pushed for time, I'll use it – and it's not bad.

Serves 4

2 roasted red peppers from a jar, well drained and roughly chopped
2 medium-hot red chillies, deseeded and roughly chopped
3 garlic cloves, roughly chopped
2 spring onions, roughly chopped
2 tablespoons white wine vinegar
1 tablespoon tomato purée
12 basil leaves
325g dried spaghetti
325g mixed cooked shellfish (prawns, mussels, squid and crab)

Place the peppers, chillies, garlic, spring onions, vinegar, tomato purée and basil in a food blender and purée until almost smooth. Season and set aside.

Meanwhile, heat a deep saucepan of salted water until boiling. Cook the spaghetti for 1 minute less than the manufacturer's instructions.

While the spaghetti is cooking, gently heat the red pepper sauce then add the seafood and warm through. Using a pasta ladle, drain the spaghetti and, with water still clinging to it, add to the seafood sauce. Toss well and serve immediately.

Tip

Don't fancy shellfish? Cut some white fish fillet into 2.5cm cubes and cook these through in the sauce before adding the pasta.

Flash-fried venison with a herb salad

Per serving
122 cals
4.5g fat
1.2g saturates
5g sugar

2g fibre
2.9g salt

1.6g fat per 100g

Venison is a meat that's reasonably low in fat but it is also tender and full of flavour. Here, I've placed it in an unusual oriental setting, showing the versatility of the game. The herb salad is deliciously refreshing.

Serves 4

2 tablespoons fish sauce
2 stalks of lemongrass, outside layer removed and roughly chopped
1 red chilli, deseeded and roughly chopped
3 spring onions, roughly chopped
1 teaspoon vegetable oil
2 garlic cloves, roughly chopped
2 teaspoons reduced-salt soy sauce
8 mint leaves
225g venison loin, thinly sliced

SALAD:

1 Baby Gem lettuce, leaves separated
1 bunch of watercress, tough stems removed
1 small bunch of mint, leaves only
1 small bunch of coriander, leaves and tender stems only
1 small bunch of dill, tougher stems removed
3 spring onions, cut into julienne
4 radishes, quartered
8 cherry tomatoes, halved
½ cucumber, peeled, deseeded and cut into 1cm pieces
½ teaspoon garlic purée
1 shallot, peeled and grated
1 tablespoon fish sauce
½ teaspoon caster sugar
1 hard-boiled egg, yolk only
1 tablespoon lime juice

In a food-processor, blend the fish sauce, lemongrass, chilli, spring onions, oil, garlic, soy sauce and mint leaves until fairly smooth. Add the venison slices to the marinade and leave for at least 2 hours, ideally overnight.

Just before cooking the venison, combine the lettuce, watercress, mint, coriander, dill, spring onions, radishes, cherry tomatoes and cucumber and arrange in a bowl.

Whisk together the garlic purée, grated shallot, fish sauce, sugar, egg yolk and lime juice and pour over the salad, tossing to combine.

Place a wok over a high heat and quickly pan-fry the venison slices for 1–3 minutes depending on how thick you've cut the venison. It should be brown on the outside and pink on the inside.

Arrange the pan-fried venison over the salad just before serving.

Main courses

Roast sea bass on Mediterranean vegetables

Loads of flavour, loads of vitamins and minerals with sea bass also providing useful pantothenic acid, a B vitamin that helps to keep the nervous system healthy, and other B vitamins, but forget all that, it's a delicious dinner party dish.

Serves 4

2 courgettes cut in 2.5cm chunks

4 spring onions, cut in half

4 garlic cloves peeled

1 red pepper, stalk and seeds removed
    cut in 2.5cm squares

16 cherry tomatoes, halved

3 sprigs thyme, leaves stripped

1 sprig rosemary, leaves stripped

1 tablespoon extra virgin olive oil

spray of olive oil

4 x 175g fillets of sea bass

1 tablespoon balsamic vinegar

6 basil leaves, ripped

Preheat the oven to 220°C/gas mark 7.

Place the first seven ingredients in a bowl and toss with the extra virgin olive oil, salt and pepper. Tip everything into a roasting tray and place in the oven for 20 minutes.

Spray a non-stick frying pan with olive oil, heat to very hot, season the sea bass fillets and place them skin side down in the pan. Sea bass tends to curl up so push the fillets flat with a fish slice. Cook them for 2 minutes to brown the skin.

Remove the roast vegetables from the oven and place the sea bass fillets skin side up on top of the vegetables. Return to the oven for 10 minutes. Lift off the fish to four warm plates then toss the vegetables with the basil leaves and the balsamic vinegar. Serve immediately with the fish.

Tip

These vegetables make a very good salad served at room temperature.

Steamed fish in lettuce and ginger

Per serving	
236 cals	2.5g fibre
5.9g fat	1.9g salt
1g saturates	
5.8g sugar	**1.9g fat per 100g**

Everyone who diets, and let's face it that seems to be most of us, needs a steamer; it doesn't need to be sophisticated, it could be just a bamboo basket set over a wok. Incidentally, when we think of steaming we must not think of hospital food – this dish has loads of flavour.

Serves 4

8 Cos lettuce leaves (the outer ones)

4 x 175g sea bass or other white fish fillets

10cm piece of root ginger, peeled and cut into very thin julienne

4 spring onions, cut into thin julienne

½ teaspoon garlic paste

2 teaspoons rice vinegar

1 teaspoon sesame oil

1 teaspoon runny honey

60ml reduced-salt soy sauce

1 medium-hot red chilli, deseeded and thinly sliced

115g frozen petits pois, defrosted

8 sticks of asparagus, trimmed and lower section peeled

Half fill a wok with water and bring to the boil. Blanch the Cos lettuce leaves for 30 seconds until they wilt. Lift out and refresh in cold water, then drain and pat dry with kitchen paper. (Reserve the boiling water for steaming later.)

Cut out the thickest part of the central rib of each lettuce leaf and lay four piles of two slightly overlapping leaves on your work surface. Place the sea bass fillets, skin side down, on the four lettuce squares. Scatter with the ginger and spring onion julienne.

Whisk together the garlic, vinegar, sesame oil, honey and soy sauce in a bowl.

Scatter a few peas over the fish, together with two sticks of asparagus. Working on one pile at a time, drizzle a little of the soy mixture over the fish then enclose with the lettuce. Place on a plate that will fit inside a bamboo steamer. Repeat with the other fish.

Place the bamboo steamer over a wok of boiling water, cover with a lid and steam for 8–10 minutes.

Serve with rice and a little more of the marinade.

Monkfish and prosciutto skewers with thyme tomatoes

Per serving

220 cals   1.1g fibre

5g fat   1.8g salt

1.4g saturates

3.1g sugar   **1.8g fat per 100g**

Monkfish is a wonderfully meaty fish which has the cooking qualities of meat and cooks well on the barbecue or griddle pan. It also contains a good quantity of the vitamin B group as well as trace minerals.

Serves 4

grated zest of 1 unwaxed lemon

1 sprig of rosemary, leaves stripped and finely chopped

¼ teaspoon ground black pepper

675g monkfish fillet, skin and cartilege removed, cut into 12 x 2.5cm pieces

6 slices prosciutto (Parma or Serrano ham), fat removed and each cut in 2 lengthways

2 garlic cloves, crushed to a paste with a little sea salt

2 sprigs of thyme, leaves stripped

2 teaspoons capers, drained, rinsed and finely chopped

4 beefsteak tomatoes, each cut into 3 horizontally

spray of olive oil

Preheat the oven to 150°C/gas mark 2.

On a flat dish combine the lemon zest, rosemary and black pepper then roll the monkfish pieces in the mix. Lay the strips of prosciutto lengthways on your work surface. Place a piece of fish at one end of each slice and roll up. Thread two rolls on each skewer (if using wood, pre-soak them in cold water for an hour), then set aside until you are ready to cook.

Meanwhile, mash together the garlic, thyme and capers. Spray each slice of tomato with olive oil, then spread with a little of the garlicky paste and sprinkle with black pepper. Cook for 1 hour, then increase the temperature to 220°C/gas mark 7 and cook for a further 10 minutes.

Heat a griddle pan, large frying pan or barbecue. Spray the skewers with a light coating of oil and cook them for 6–7 minutes over a medium heat, turning once.

Serve a piece of fish on each slice of tomato, accompanied by a green salad.

Tip

While the tomatoes are slow-cooking, the fish will marinate nicely with the lemon and rosemary.

Poached haddock in a herb and tomato broth

Per serving

222 cals   1.3g fibre

8.8g fat   2.3g salt

4.4g saturates

6.4g sugar   **2.4g fat per 100g**

This is a delicate way to cook fish that is also extremely healthy. The broth has flavours reminiscent of salsa verde but without so much oil. Serve with new potatoes.

Serves 4

2 teaspoons olive oil

1 red onion, finely diced

1 garlic clove, finely chopped

2 sprigs of thyme, leaves stripped

½ teaspoon toasted fennel seeds

2 anchovy fillets, rinsed, drained and chopped

2 teaspoons Lilliput (baby) capers

2 cornichons, finely chopped

2 teaspoons Worcestershire sauce

400ml dashi, fish or vegetable stock

4 x 175g fillets of haddock

3 tomatoes, deseeded and diced

3 tablespoons finely chopped parsley

In a large saucepan, over a medium heat, cook the onion with the olive oil for 6–8 minutes, then add the garlic, thyme, fennel seeds and anchovies and cook gently for a further 3 minutes.

Add the capers, cornichons, Worcestershire sauce and stock and bring to the boil. Cook for 5 minutes then add the fillets of fish, cook for 5 minutes more, then fold in the tomatoes and parsley. Season and serve in bowls.

Tip

This dish also works well with monkfish, sea bass, brill, turbot, halibut and sea bream.

A butter bean stew

Per serving

210 cals   7.4g fibre

3.1g fat   0.4g salt

0.8g saturates

12.3g sugar   **0.8g fat per 100g**

Serves 4

2 teaspoons olive oil

2 onions, roughly chopped

6 garlic cloves, roughly chopped

2 sticks of celery, thinly sliced

1 carrot, thinly sliced

1 teaspoon fennel seeds

¼ teaspoon ground cinnamon

1 teaspoon dried oregano

1 teaspoon caster sugar

1 x 400g tin chopped tomatoes

2 teaspoons tomato purée

2 x 400g tins butter beans, drained and rinsed

115g low-fat cottage cheese

2 teaspoons chopped fresh oregano

Heat the olive oil in a saucepan then add the onions and cook for 10 minutes over a medium heat so as to soften but not brown them. Add the garlic, celery, carrot and fennel seeds and cook over a medium heat for a further 3 minutes.

Add the cinnamon, oregano, sugar, tinned tomatoes and tomato purée and stir to combine. Bring to the boil, then reduce the heat and simmer for 25 minutes.

Add the beans and cook for a further 15 minutes. Serve into four warm bowls then crumble over the cottage cheese and fresh oregano.

Tip

This stew works well with all sorts of tinned beans, not including the baked variety.

Per serving

330 cals	3.3g fibre
11.9g fat	1.5g salt
2.4g saturates	
3.1g sugar	**3g fat per 100g**

Swordfish with citrus notes

Swordfish, like tuna and marlin are very meaty fish that don't benefit from being overcooked. The topping works well with the citrus flavours cutting through the richness of the fish.

Serves 4

450g new potatoes
325g broccoli florets
4 x 175g swordfish steaks
spray of olive oil

CITRUS SALSA:

1 tablespoon extra virgin olive oil
juice and grated zest of 1 unwaxed lemon
juice and grated zest of ½ navel orange
1 mild long red chilli, deseeded and
    finely diced
2 spring onions, finely chopped
1 garlic clove, finely chopped
1½ tablespoons Lilliput (baby) capers,
    rinsed and drained
8 pitted Kalamata olives in brine, rinsed
    and finely chopped
1 tablespoon chopped mint
2 teaspoons snipped chives

Combine the salsa ingredients in a bowl and leave the flavours to develop for 20 minutes. Season to taste.

Meanwhile, in a pan of boiling water, cook the new potatoes for 12–15 minutes until nearly tender, then add the broccoli and cook for a further 4 minutes. Carefully drain and season. Keep warm.

Heat a griddle pan or large frying pan until almost smoking. Season the swordfish with salt and pepper and spray a fine mist of olive oil over the surface of the fish. Cook over a fierce heat for 1 minute each side. Turn off the heat and allow the steaks to sit for 3 minutes in the residual heat.

Serve with the broccoli and new potatoes, with the citrus salsa scattered over the fish.

Roast butternut squash with Chinese influence

Per serving
162 cal   5.7g fibre
0.5g fat   3.9g salt
0.1g saturates
22g sugar   **0.1g fat per 100**

One of my favourite vegetables of all time. I use it in all sorts of guises but I particularly like it roasted, as here, as the Chinese flavours give it a lovely richness. Roasting doesn't have to mean using oil – this dish is completely free from added fat but still looks and tastes amazing.

Serves 4

3 small red onions, cut in rough
   chunks or wedges
12 garlic cloves, left whole and peeled
120ml vegetable stock
1 large butternut squash, peeled,
   deseeded and cut into 4cm chunks
3 tablespoons soy sauce
3 tablespoons Chinese oyster sauce
1 tablespoon sweet chilli sauce
1 tablespoon lime juice
1 tablespoon honey
2 tablespoons ripped basil leaves,
   ideally Thai
2 tablespoons coriander leaves

TO SERVE:

red chilli slices
lime wedges
brown rice

Preheat the oven to 190°C/gas mark 5.

Toss the onions, garlic and vegetables stock together and place in a deep roasting tray. Place the tray in the oven and cook for 40–50 minutes until the butternut squash is fork tender.

Meanwhile combine the soy sauce, oyster sauce, chilli sauce, lime juice and honey in a bowl. Pour the mixture over the squash, stir to combine and return to the oven for 5 minutes.

Decant to a serving dish and sprinkle with the herbs and sliced chillies. Serve as a meal with brown rice or as an accompaniment to fish or chicken.

Tip

This recipe will work with all varieties of the squash and pumpkin family.

Chilli non carne

Per serving (based on 6 portions)

301 cals   8.1g fibre

5g fat   2.4g salt

0.8g saturates

13.2g sugar   **1.1g fat per 100g**

Everyone loves a chilli so there's no reason why low-fat vegetarians shouldn't get involved in the chilli process. You're looking for all the flavours without the meat thereby achieving your low-fat targets at the same time. Feel free to use different vegetables as long as you're sticking to the flavour base. This is a real store-cupboard recipe.

Serves 4–6

150g quinoa or bulgur wheat

270ml water, very hot

2 teaspoons olive oil

1 onion, roughly chopped

3 garlic cloves, crushed to a paste with a little salt

2 green chillies, deseeded and finely chopped

1 stick celery, finely chopped

1 bay leaf

1 teaspoon dried oregano

1 teaspoon ground cumin

1 teaspoon ground coriander

1 teaspoon sweet paprika

½ teaspoon cayenne pepper

½ teaspoon ground fennel

½ teaspoon ground cinnamon

2 x 400g tins of chopped tomatoes

450ml vegetable stock

1 x 400g tin red kidney beans, drained and rinsed

1 x 400g tin cannellini beans, drained and rinsed

1 x 400g tin chickpeas, drained and rinsed

1 x 326g tin sweetcorn, drained

1 teaspoon cocoa powder

2 tablespoons chopped coriander leaves

Put the quinoa in a bowl and pour over the hot water and allow to soak for 12 minutes.

In a large saucepan, heat the olive oil and gently cook the onion for 8–10 minutes until softened but not coloured. Add the garlic, chillies and celery and cook for a further 2 minutes. Fold in the herbs and spices and stir to combine.

Add the tinned tomatoes, stock and quinoa and stir. Over a medium heat bring to the boil, reduce the heat and cook gently for 20 minutes. Add all of the canned vegetables and cook gently for 15 minutes. Fold in the cocoa and coriander and season to taste.

Serve piping hot with 0% fat Greek yogurt, some diced raw tomatoes and red onion and some tortilla chips.

Mixed vegetable burger

Per serving
358 cals
4.4g fat
1.3g saturates
10g sugar

4g fibre
1.1g salt

1.3g fat per 100g

As a vegetarian you still want to enjoy some frivolous food, but why not make the burger yourself rather than buy something that appears to have been manufactured by a scientist? Whether you're a vegetarian or not, these are delicious and they are a great source of fibre, folate, potassium and antioxidants.

Serves 4

1 x 400g tin flageolet beans or
   cannellini beans, drained and rinsed
spray of olive oil
1 onion, finely chopped
3 garlic cloves, mashed to a paste
   with a little salt
2 green chillies, deseeded and
   finely chopped
1 teaspoon ground cumin
½ teaspoon ground coriander
½ teaspoon ground fennel
1 courgette, grated
½ red pepper, deseeded and cut
   into 1cm dice
2 spring onions, finely sliced
85g soft fresh breadcrumbs
1 tablespoon wholewheat flour
55g ricotta cheese

TO SERVE:

4 pitta bread, toasted
handful of salad leaves or rocket
1 beefsteak tomato, cut into 4 slices
4 tablespoons 0% fat Greek yogurt
   (optional)

In a large bowl, mash the beans with a fork or potato masher, retaining a little texture.

Spray a frying pan with oil and cook the onion over a medium heat for 6–8 minutes until softened but without colour. Add the garlic paste, chillies and spices and cook for a further 3 minutes, stirring regularly. Allow to cool.

Add the courgette, red pepper, spring onions, breadcrumbs and flour to the onions and use your hands to combine the mixture, squeezing to compress the ingredients together. Divide the mixture into four.

Take one ball in your hands and flatten to create a burger shape. Make an indent with your thumb and place a quarter of the ricotta in the well, bringing the mixture over to enclose the cheese. Repeat with the other three. Ideally refrigerate for a couple of hours to firm up the burgers.

Using a frying pan sprayed with oil, cook the burgers for 3–4 minutes on each side or until golden brown. Once brown, you could finish them in the oven (preheated to 180°C/gas mark 4) if you wanted.

Cut the pitta in half horizontally, fill with the salad and tomato slices, followed by the burger and, if desired, a dollop of yogurt.

Veal escalopes with prosciutto and basil

Per serving
272 cals   2.1g fibre
9g fat   1.3g salt
2.2g saturates
6.6g sugar   **2.5g fat per 100g**

This dish, based loosely on veal saltimbocca, is a simple, no-hassle dinner party-style dish. Some of you, like me, will be concerned about the welfare of veal calves, but in the UK we can now buy rose veal, which is reared in a humane way; its flesh is not as white as that of traditional veal but the flavour is better. Alternatively, you could substitute pork tenderloin or beaten-out chicken breast, but veal is a low-fat meat.

Serves 4

4 x 115g rose veal escalopes,
   beaten thin
8 basil leaves
4 slices of prosciutto (Parma or
   Serrano ham), any fat removed
1 tablespoon olive oil
1 garlic clove, lightly crushed
1 whole dried red chilli
seasoned plain flour, for coating
120ml dry white wine

FOR THE SALAD:

8 tomatoes on the vine, quartered
½ red onion, finely sliced
8 basil leaves, ripped
2 teaspoons extra virgin olive oil
1 tablespoon balsamic vinegar

Lay the veal escalopes on your work surface, top each with two basil leaves, season, then top with the prosciutto, pressing down to create a seal.

Heat the oil in a large frying pan with the garlic and chilli, and cook until the garlic is golden and the chilli has darkened, turning both from time to time; the oil should not be too hot, the idea being to release the flavour of the garlic and chilli rather than burn them. Discard the solids.

Dust the escalopes on both sides with seasoned flour then place them, prosciutto-side down, into the flavoured oil. Cook for 2 minutes over a medium heat, then turn them over and cook for a further 2 minutes. Remove and set aside to keep warm.

Meanwhile, for the salad, combine all the ingredients and season to taste.

Pour the wine into the frying pan and stir well to loosen any meat residue from the bottom of the pan. Season, then pour over the escalopes and serve immediately.

Tip

Some like to secure the ham to the veal with cocktail sticks, but this is not necessary, if you are careful when you turn the escalopes over. Always cook the ham side of the veal first.

Asian chicken, rice and peas

Per serving

387 cals   3.8g fibre

8.9g fat   2.9g salt

1.7g saturates

14.1g sugar   **1.8g fat per 100g**

I'm a fan of the chicken and rice you see all over Singapore which inspired this little number; it's simple, very tasty and good value.

Serves 4

1 tablespoon rapeseed or vegetable oil

2 large onions, thinly sliced

1 teaspoon chopped garlic

1 teaspoon grated ginger

3 teaspoons dashi stock powder

300ml boiling water

30ml Japanese soy sauce

90ml mirin (Japanese cooking wine)

1 tablespoon liquid honey

2 large chicken breasts, thinly sliced

175g sugar snap peas, topped and tailed

6 shiitake mushrooms, stems removed and quartered

2 free-range eggs, lightly beaten

325g easy-cook, 2-minute brown rice

4 spring onions, thinly sliced on the diagonal

2 long green chillies, deseeded and thinly sliced

Heat the oil in a large saucepan and cook the onions gently for 15 minutes. Increase the temperature, add the garlic and ginger and cook for a further 5 minutes to lightly brown the onions.

Whisk the dashi powder in the boiling water, then add the soy sauce, mirin and honey and simmer for 5 minutes before adding the onion mixture.

Add the chicken, sugar snaps and mushrooms and cook for 5 minutes with the liquid boiling. Pour in the beaten eggs in a steady stream, stirring the liquid as you do to create egg strands.

Cook the rice either in your microwave, or according to the instructions on the packet. Spoon into four bowls, then top with the chicken and egg broth. Garnish with the spring onions and chillies.

Tip

Many supermarkets sell dashi stock nowadays, oriental markets certainly do, but if you can't find it just substitute chicken stock.

Braised cod with spices
and tomatoes

Per serving
282 cals   3.2g fibre
4.7g fat   0.9g salt
0.6g saturates
10.2g sugar   **1g fat per 100g**

This is a delicious way to serve white fish, and also makes an excellent dinner-party dish. By now we all know how good cooked tomatoes are for us, so with the added benefits of fish you can eat without guilt. Serve with brown rice.

Serves 4

55g seasoned white flour
4 x 175g cod fillets
1 tablespoon vegetable oil
1 onion, finely diced
1 fennel bulb, outside layer removed,
     the remainder finely chopped
3 garlic cloves, crushed to a paste
     with a little salt
½ teaspoon chilli powder
1 teaspoon ground coriander
1 teaspoon ground cumin
1 teaspoon ground turmeric
1 x 400g tin chopped tomatoes
1 teaspoon caster sugar
150ml 0% fat Greek yogurt
1 teaspoon garam masala
3 tomatoes, roughly chopped
2 mild green chillies, deseeded and
     roughly chopped
handful of baby spinach, washed

Preheat the oven to 220°C/gas mark 7.

Place the flour on a plate then dip in the cod to cover both sides, shaking off any excess.

Heat the oil in an ovenproof frying pan over a high heat, brown the cod on both sides, remove and set aside.

Into the same pan, add the onion, fennel and garlic and cook gently for 10–12 minutes until the vegetables have softened but have little or no colour. Add all the spices (not the garam masala) and cook for 2 minutes.

Add the tinned tomatoes and sugar, increase the heat and cook for 10 minutes to thicken, then fold in the yogurt and stir to combine. Return the cod to the pan together with the garam masala, chopped tomatoes and chillies. Cover and place in the oven and cook for 12 minutes.

Remove from the oven, take out the cod fillets and keep warm in a serving dish. Add the spinach to the sauce and cook until wilted. Check the seasoning then spoon over the cod and serve.

Chicken and bacon dal

Per serving

365 cals   7.4g fibre

7.7g fat   2g salt

1.5g saturates

6.4g sugar   **2.8g fat per 100g**

I know that dal dishes are normally associated with vegetarianism, but I reckon they're great for meat dishes as well. Serve this with a salad.

Serves 4

275g yellow split peas, rinsed

1 teaspoon ground turmeric

1 teaspoon ground cumin

1 teaspoon ground coriander

¼ teaspoon ground fennel

1 teaspoon salt

½ teaspoon ground white pepper

4 curry leaves

1 tablespoon vegetable oil

2 rashers smoked back bacon, visible fat removed

4 skinless, boneless chicken thighs, each cut into three

1 onion, finely chopped

4 garlic cloves, crushed to a paste with a little salt

1 teaspoon grated ginger

1 teaspoon brown mustard seeds

150g extra fine French beans

¼ Savoy cabbage, finely shredded

½ teaspoon garam masala

3 spring onions, finely sliced

1 mild green chilli, deseeded and finely sliced (optional)

Put the split peas in a saucepan and cover with 2.5cm water. Bring to the boil, reduce the heat and simmer for 5 minutes.

Add the turmeric, cumin, coriander, fennel, salt, pepper and curry leaves, then cover with a lid and simmer for 1 hour, skimming off any scum from time to time. Make sure that the split peas are tender but haven't completely collapsed.

Meanwhile, 20 minutes before the end of the dal cooking time, heat the oil in a wok or saucepan then add the bacon and chicken and cook over a medium heat for 8 minutes. Remove and set aside to keep warm.

Add the onion, garlic, ginger and mustard seeds to the chicken pan and cook gently for 10 minutes before adding the beans, cabbage and 3 tablespoons of water. Cook for 2 minutes then return the chicken and bacon to the pan, together with the split pea mixture. Stir to combine then fold in the garam masala and check the seasoning.

Scatter the surface with spring onions, and chilli, if desired.

Lamb stew on the quick

Per serving

420 cals   3.2g fibre

12.6g fat   0.6g salt

5.1g saturates

4.8g sugar   **2.9g fat per 100g**

This is so simple but so tasty, and it's literally going to take you minutes to have supper on the table. Lamb is not cheap nowadays so I've gone for one of its best-value cuts, but you will have to slice it thinly to save your molars. Serve with new potatoes.

Serves 6

450g lamb neck fillets, trimmed
  of any sinews or fat

spray of olive oil

1 onion, finely diced

4 garlic cloves, crushed to a paste with
  a little salt

1 tablespoon toasted cumin seeds

3 anchovy fillets, roughly chopped

a pinch of chilli flakes

½ teaspoon ground rosemary or very
  finely chopped rosemary needles

180ml white wine

1 x 400g tin chopped tomatoes

1 x 400g tin flageolet beans, drained
  and rinsed

2 tablespoons chopped parsley

450g pappardelle or other large pasta

Cut the lamb fillet crossways into 5mm slices across the grain, spray with a fine film of oil then fry in a large frying pan over a high heat for 1 minute each side. Remove and set aside to keep warm. You may have to fry in batches to accommodate all the slices.

In the same pan, cook the onion over a medium heat for 8–10 minutes, without it colouring too much, then add the garlic, cumin, anchovy, chilli and rosemary. Stir to combine and cook for a further 3 minutes until the anchovy breaks down.

Add the white wine and boil vigorously until most of the liquor has evaporated, then add the tomatoes and cook for 10 minutes. Add the beans along with the lamb and any accumulated juices. Heat through for 5 minutes but do not let it boil. Season and fold in the parsley.

Meanwhile cook the pasta according to the manufacturer's instructions and serve with the stew.

Tip

This recipe works equally well with chicken or pork fillet, although you may have to cook the meat for a little longer depending on how thick you cut it.

Cajun prawns with green beans and coriander

Per serving

124 cals	2.4g fibre
4.3g fat	1.8g salt
0.5g saturates	
9.5g sugar	**2g fat per 100g**

I love Cajun spice mixes, and this blend works well with other shellfish, white fish, chicken or pork; you can make the paste in larger quantities if you like. The prawns go well with rice or new potatoes, and they also make a great filling for a tortilla wrap or as a topping for pancakes.

Serves 4

CAJUN PASTE:

1 tablespoon sweet paprika

1 teaspoon onion salt

1 teaspoon garlic salt

1 teaspoon chilli or cayenne powder

½ teaspoon ground ginger

2 tablespoons ground cumin

1 teaspoon ground coriander

1 teaspoon ground cardamom

1 red onion, roughly chopped

1 tablespoon vegetable oil

3 garlic cloves, roughly chopped

24 raw tiger prawns, shell off, deveined

175g haricots verts (green beans), cut
 into 2.5cm pieces

spray of vegetable oil

8 cherry tomatoes, halved

1 red onion, finely sliced

juice and grated zest of 1 lime

2 teaspoons runny honey

½ bunch of coriander, leaves only

For the Cajun paste, simply blend all the ingredients in a food-processor. Thin half the paste with a little water and use to marinate the prawns, tossing to combine. Leave covered for 20 minutes.

Cook the beans in plenty of boiling, salted water for 4 minutes. Drain, discard the water and set aside.

Spray a large frying pan with oil, add the remaining paste and fry until fragrant, about 2 minutes, stirring continuously. Add the prawns and cook for 2 minutes. Then add the tomatoes and onion and cook for a further 2 minutes, stirring regularly.

Fold in the beans, lime juice and zest, honey and coriander and toss to combine. Cook for 1–2 minutes until everything is piping hot.

Smoked haddock and salmon biryani

Per serving
411 cals
13.6g fat
6g saturates
15.4g sugar

3.6g fibre
2.4g salt

3g fat per 100g

This recipe is loosely based on kedgeree, but with a few more Indian spices added and a different cooking technique. It's a lovely one-pot dinner-party dish that has loads of flavour. All you need is a salad to go with it.

Serves 6

1 tablespoon vegetable oil
2 onions, finely chopped
4 garlic cloves, crushed to a paste
  with a little salt
1 teaspoon grated ginger
1 teaspoon ground coriander
1 teaspoon ground cumin
2 green cardamom pods, lightly crushed
2.5cm cinnamon stick
1 teaspoon ground turmeric
½ teaspoon chilli powder
1 teaspoon yellow mustard seeds
225g long-grain or basmati rice, rinsed
600ml chicken or fish stock
300ml reduced-fat coconut milk
300ml 0% fat Greek yogurt
115g frozen petits pois, defrosted
1 large courgette, finely sliced
115g dried apricots, finely chopped
225g natural smoked haddock fillets,
  skin removed, cut into 2.5cm dice
200g salmon fillet, cut into 2.5cm dice
2 tablespoons chopped coriander,
  leaf and stalk
2 green chillies, deseeded and
  thinly sliced

Preheat the oven to 190°C/gas mark 5.

In an ovenproof saucepan with a lid, heat the oil over a medium heat then add the onion, garlic and ginger and cook gently for 10 minutes, stirring from time to time.

Add all the spices and stir to combine, cooking for 1 minute. Weigh the rice then measure it using a cup as you add it to the pan with the spiced onions. Then measure one and half times as much stock as rice, and add this to the pan as well. Bring to the boil, cover with a circle of parchment paper, then a lid, and pop in the oven for 15 minutes. When it's ready, stir through with a fork.

Meanwhile, bring the coconut milk and yogurt to the boil in a pan, then reduce the heat and add the peas, courgette, apricots and the two fish. Cook for 6–8 minutes. Season, then fold in the coriander and green chillies.

Fold the fish mixture into the rice and check the seasoning.

Roast butternut squash, leek and tomato risotto

Per serving
296 cals   8.1g fibre
4g fat   1.8g salt
0.9g saturates
15.5g sugar   **0.7g fat per 100g**

Risotto needs cheese, or does it? I found that, by adding a vegetable purée, we can compensate for the lack of a cheesy flavour. This recipe allows for many vegetable options.

Serves 6

1 small butternut squash, peeled, deseeded and cut into 2.5cm dice
4 sprigs of thyme
½ head of garlic, cloves separated but unpeeled
2 onions, peeled and cut into 8 wedges
spray of olive oil
750ml vegetable stock
2 teaspoons olive oil
2 sticks of celery, finely sliced
1 carrot, peeled and finely diced
1 bay leaf
225g arborio rice
2 leeks, washed and shredded finely
115g frozen broad beans, defrosted
115g frozen petits pois, defrosted
3 tomatoes, deseeded and finely diced

Preheat the oven to 200°C/gas mark 6.

Put the butternut squash, thyme, garlic and onions in a bowl and spray with olive oil. Toss to coat then season and put into a roasting tray and cook for 30 minutes, stirring from time to time.

Meanwhile, heat the stock to boiling in one saucepan.

In another, heat the oil then add the celery, carrot and bay leaf. Cook gently for 10–12 minutes to soften the vegetables. Add the rice and half the leeks and toss to combine. Add one ladleful of stock and, stirring constantly, cook until the liquid has all but evaporated and been soaked up by the rice. Then add another and so on until the rice is tender, about 18–20 minutes.

Meanwhile, when the squash is cooked, remove from the oven, pop the garlic out of their skins, then put half of the roast vegetables and garlic into a food-processor and blend until smooth.

Eight minutes before the risotto has finished cooking, add the purée to the pan, together with the rest of the roast vegetables, the remaining leeks, broad beans and peas. Two minutes before the end of cooking, add the diced tomatoes and season to taste.

Tip

It's important, to obtain the risotto's distinctive creamy texture, to add the stock little by little. If you're not sure whether the rice is cooked, just take a teaspoon and try it; you're looking for a tiny bite to the rice.

Pork with celeriac and apple mash

Per serving

283 cals	6.9g fibre
8.1g fat	1g salt
1.9g saturates	
10.6g sugar	**1.8g fat per 100g**

I've always been a massive fan of pork, which is a low-fat meat, and the combination of celeriac and apples creates a perfect partnership. Celeriac is an underused vegetable, partly I'm sure because of the look, which tends to scare all but the keenest cook; the best thing is to think of celeriac simply as a knobbly potato and to cook it in the same way.

Serves 6

1 tablespoon olive oil

675g pork fillets (tenderloin), trimmed of any fat

1 tablespoon Dijon mustard

1 tablespoon redcurrant jelly

175ml red wine

1 celeriac, peeled and cut into 2.5cm dice

2 floury potatoes, peeled and cut into 2.5cm dice

2 Bramley apples, peeled, cored and cut into 2.5cm dice

1 tablespoon yellow mustard seeds

120ml chicken stock

2 teaspoons finely chopped sage leaves

Preheat the oven to 200°C/gas mark 6.

Heat the oil in a frying pan and brown the pork all over. Remove from the pan and allow to cool slightly before painting all over with Dijon mustard. Place in the oven and cook for 15–20 minutes.

Meanwhile, add the redcurrant jelly and wine to the pork browning pan and simmer gently until the jelly melts.

At the same time, place the celeriac, potatoes and apple in a pan of boiling salted water and cook for 12–15 minutes, until the potato and celeriac are tender. Drain and dry well, then mash, pass through a fine sieve or a mouli-legumes or pulse in a food-processor until smooth. Set aside and keep warm.

Meanwhile, it's back to the sauce. Add the mustard seeds, chicken stock and sage to the red wine reduction and cook until reduced by one-third. Season.

Remove the pork from the oven and allow to rest for at least 5 minutes. Scrape any juices from the roasting tray into the sauce. Carve the pork into thick slices on the diagonal. Serve the sauce spooned over the pork alongside a nice dollop of celeriac and apple mash.

Tip

If preparing the celeriac and apple in advance, place the raw, peeled dice in acidulated water until ready to cook, to stop them going brown.

Pearl barley and wild mushroom pilaff

Per serving

414 cals   2.8g fibre
5.3g fat   2.2g salt
1g saturates
4.9g sugar   **1.1g fat per 100g**

I love the texture of pearl barley. It has a lovely feel about it and makes a low-GI substitute for rice. It's often used in soups and stews, but you now see pearl barley more regularly in dishes like this and risotto.

Serves 4

300g pearl barley, washed and soaked in cold water for 1 hour

25g dried cep mushrooms (porcini), soaked in boiling water for 30 minutes

1 tablespoon olive oil

1 onion, finely chopped

2 garlic cloves, crushed to a paste with a little salt

1 teaspoon thyme leaves

2 bay leaves

1 celery stick, finely chopped

1 carrot, peeled and cut into 5mm dice

450ml vegetable stock

300ml red wine

400g mixed wild mushrooms, cleaned and cut in half if too large

1 teaspoon ground black pepper

2 teaspoons Maggi seasoning (optional)

2 handfuls of baby spinach leaves, washed

Drain the pearl barley and set aside.

Carefully remove the soaked ceps without disturbing the soaking liquor too much. Roughly chop the mushrooms and set aside. Strain the mushroom soaking liquor through a coffee filter, muslin or a very fine sieve to remove any gritty particles, then set aside.

Preheat the oven to 180°C/gas mark 4.

Heat the oil in an ovenproof saucepan and cook the onion over a medium heat for 8–10 minutes until softened. Add the garlic, thyme, bay leaves, celery and carrot and cook for a further 3 minutes.

Meanwhile, heat the vegetable stock and red wine with the reserved mushroom liquor until just below boiling point.

Add both the fresh and soaked mushrooms to the onion mixture and cook over a high heat for 3 minutes. Add the barley, black pepper and heated stock, stir to combine then bring to the boil, cover and place in the preheated oven for 35 minutes. By this stage, all the liquor should have been absorbed.

Take out of the oven, remove the lid and, over a very low heat, stir in the Maggi seasoning, if using, and the baby spinach. Stir until the spinach has wilted. Check the seasoning then serve piping hot.

Tip

I'm a great fan of Maggi liquid seasoning in soups and stews. It's like a vegetarian version of Worcestershire sauce, and adds that little *je ne sais quoi*, but, beware, it does contain MSG.

Vegetable tagine

Per serving
301 cals   9.6g fibre
9.3g fat   1.8g salt
1.2g saturates
27.1g sugar   **1.6g fat per 100g**

Ever since I filmed a TV series in Morocco I've been hooked on their use of spices and here we turn humble vegetables into a sumptuous vegetarian feast.

Serves 8

2 teaspoons olive oil

450g onion, half grated and half cut into chunky dice

½ head of garlic, peeled and crushed with salt

½ tablespoon ground ginger

½ teaspoon ground black pepper

½ teaspoon ground cinnamon

175g dried apricots, soaked in a little water

85g flaked almonds

55g sultanas or raisins

1 teaspoon liquid honey

600ml tomato juice

600ml vegetable stock

280g potatoes, peeled and cut into 2.5cm chunks

2 green peppers, deseeded and cut into 2.5cm chunks

280g pumpkin or butternut squash, peeled, deseeded and cut into 2.5cm chunks

1 x 400g tin chopped tomatoes

1 x 400g tin chickpeas, drained and rinsed

2 large courgettes, cut into 2.5cm chunks

280g cauliflower florets

280g fresh or frozen peas

25g chopped coriander

Heat the olive oil in a large, ovenproof casserole dish. When it's hot, add the grated onion, garlic and spices and gently cook until the onions are soft and translucent, about 6–8 minutes. Take care not to brown the onions or scorch the spices.

Add the remaining onions, apricots and their soaking water, the almonds, raisins or sultanas, honey, tomato juice and vegetable stock. Bring to the boil, reduce the heat and allow to simmer until the sauce has reduced by a third.

Add the vegetables in order of cooking time: start with the potatoes and green peppers and gently cook for approximately 12 minutes, then add the pumpkin or squash, tinned tomatoes and chickpeas, cook for 8 minutes, then add the courgettes, cauliflower florets and the peas. Continue to cook until all the vegetables are tender, about a further 10 minutes.

Serve immediately, sprinkled with coriander.

Roast lemon chicken with root vegetables

Per serving

409 cals   7.4g fibre

13.5g fat   0.6g salt

3.4g saturates

17.1g sugar   **2.4g fat per 100g**

There is a bit of a dilemma here as most of the fat is in the chicken skin, which will be reduced by roasting, rendering the skin very crispy and very delicious – but you know better, so remove the skin before carving and drain all the fat from the roasting juices. This is easily done if you have a fat separator gravy jug, otherwise pour the juices into a glass jug, which will enable you to see the fats and skim them off; you can fish out any small bubbles by dragging a piece of absorbent kitchen paper over the surface.

Serves 4

grated zest and juice of 1 unwaxed
    lemon

2 garlic cloves, crushed to a paste with
    a little rock salt

3 sprigs of rosemary, 1 stripped of its
    leaves and finely chopped

pinch of chilli flakes

$^1/_8$ teaspoon ground black pepper

1 x 1.5kg free-range roasting chicken,
    (skin removed after cooking)

12 baby onions, peeled

½ butternut squash (approx. 350g),
    peeled, deseeded and cut into
    2cm dice

12 baby carrots (approx. 300g),
    scrubbed

8 baby leeks (approx. 400g), washed
    and trimmed

8 new potatoes (approx. 200g), halved

6 baby courgettes (approx. 300g),
    halved lengthways

2 teaspoons olive oil

Preheat the oven to 200°C/gas mark 6.

Mash the lemon zest and juice with the garlic, chopped rosemary leaves, chilli and black pepper, and spread over and inside the chicken.

In a bowl, combine all the vegetables with the oil and season with salt and ground black pepper. Tip them into a roasting tray and make a little well in the centre, and place the chicken in this well.

Cook the chicken and vegetables in the oven for 1¼ hours, turning the vegetables regularly. Remove the chicken to a warm place and allow to rest for 15 minutes. With a slotted spoon, lift the vegetables into a serving bowl.

Skim off any fat from the roasting juices and add 4 tablespoons of water to the roasting tray. Stir to remove any pan residue and pour these juices over the carved chicken and serve with the vegetables.

Tip

Feel free to mix and match the variety of vegetables, making sure that you keep them roughly the same size. If using large carrots, blanch them first for 8–10 minutes.

Roast fillet of spiced pork with colourful vegetables

Per serving
403 cals   7.1g fibre
7.1g fat   4.6g salt
2.2g saturates
28.5g sugar   **1.1g fat per 100g**

Pork fillet is still very good value for a quality cut and it takes big flavours, which is what this dish is about – that and some lovely roast vegetables, of course.

Serves 4

2 x centre-cut pork fillets, each about 225g, trimmed of any fat or sinews

6 tablespoons kecap manis (Indonesian soy sauce)

2 tablespoons mirin or dry sherry

1 teaspoon five spice powder

¼ teaspoon red food colouring (optional)

2 garlic cloves, crushed to a paste with a little salt

1 teaspoon hot chilli sauce

1 teaspoon grated ginger

THE VEGETABLES:

1 red pepper, deseeded and cut into 2.5cm pieces

½ butternut squash, peeled, deseeded and cut into 2.5cm pieces

8 new potatoes, halved

2 courgettes, cut into 2.5cm rings

1 leek, washed and cut into 2.5cm rings

1 red onion, peeled and cut into 8 wedges

spray of vegetable oil

8 garlic cloves, unpeeled

2 tablespoons rice vinegar

2 tablespoons caster sugar

Place the pork fillets in a shallow dish. In a separate bowl, stir together the kecap manis, mirin, five spice, red food colouring (if using), garlic, chilli sauce and grated ginger. Pour over the pork and marinate for 4 hours, turning from time to time.

Preheat the oven to 190°C/gas mark 5.

Place all the vegetables in a bowl and spray with oil and season with salt and pepper. Mix well then put in a roasting tray and top with the pork fillet. Place in the oven and roast for 50 minutes, adding the garlic cloves after 20 minutes. During the cooking, baste every so often with the marinade.

Remove the meat and rest in a warm place, then toss the vegetables in the vinegar and sugar and return to the oven for 8 minutes.

Carve the pork and serve on a platter of the roast vegetables.

Spiced salmon and prawns with yogurt and white beans

Salmon is such a good vehicle for transporting strong flavours, here I've gone for some Moroccan influence, with all you require on one plate.

Serves 4

3 garlic cloves, crushed to a paste
   with a little salt

1 tablespoon ground coriander

1 teaspoon ground cumin

1 teaspoon ground fennel

1 teaspoon ground turmeric

1 tablespoon olive oil

1 tablespoon water

16 raw tiger prawns, peeled

85g salmon fillets

2 x 400g tin white beans, drained

½ cucumber, peeled and deseeded
   and cut into ½cm dice

1 tablespoon chopped mint

3 tablespoons chopped coriander

180ml 0% fat free Greek style yogurt

spray of olive oil

8 cherry tomatoes halved horizontally

Combine the garlic with the spices, oil and water to make a paste. Rub the prawns and the salmon fillets with half the paste, massaging it well into the flesh. Allow the flavours to develop for 20 minutes.

Meanwhile, mix the remaining paste with the white beans, cucumber, mint, coriander and yogurt.

Spray a non-stick frying pan with a film of oil, pan-fry the salmon for 2 minutes on each side, remove and set aside to keep warm, then repeat with the prawns, cooking for 1 minute each side. Add to the salmon, to keep warm.

To the fish pan add the bean mix and cook for 5 minutes to warm through.

Serve the salmon and the prawns on a bed of beans and scatter each plate with 4 tomato halves.

Tip

This would be a lovely picnic dish – cook the salmon and prawns in the normal way and allow to cool. There is no need to cook the beans.

Spicy prawn balls in a tomato and coriander sauce

Per serving
245 cals   3.1g fibre
3.3g fat   2.8g salt
0.5g saturates
13.7g sugar   **0.6g fat per 100g**

Always try to eat at least two portions of fish each week, which is easier said than done according to the statistics. This dish uses prawns that are now exceptional value for a fairly luxurious item. I would serve this with spaghetti or rice.

Serves 4

SAUCE:

2 x 400g tins chopped tomatoes

2 teaspoons olive oil

1 onion, finely chopped

3 garlic cloves, crushed to a paste
    with a little salt

3 small dried chillies

juice and zest of 1 orange

12 cherry tomatoes

½ bunch of coriander, roughly
    chopped

2 handfuls of baby spinach, washed

2 teaspoons caster sugar

1 tablespoon nam pla (fish sauce)

PRAWN BALLS:

675g raw prawns, peeled, tail off,
    deveined and roughly chopped

2 garlic cloves, roughly chopped

3 small red Thai chillies, roughly
    chopped

1 teaspoon ground ginger

grated zest and juice of 1 lime

2 tablespoons chopped coriander

5 spring onions, roughly chopped

2 tablespoons chopped mint

1 tablespoon cornflour

1 tablespoon nam pla

1 egg white, lightly beaten

For the sauce, blend the tinned tomatoes in a food-processor until smooth. Set aside.

Heat the oil in a saucepan then, over a medium heat, cook the onion, garlic and chillies for 8–10 minutes until soft but not coloured. Add the orange juice and zest and continue to cook until most of the liquid has evaporated. Add the puréed tomatoes, bring to the boil, then reduce the heat and simmer for 12 minutes.

To make the prawn balls, pulse the chopped prawns with the garlic, chilli, ginger, lime juice and zest in a food-processor until semi-smooth but with some texture remaining. Transfer the prawn mixture to a bowl, add the coriander, spring onion, mint, cornflour, nam pla and egg white, and mix thoroughly.

With wet hands, roll the mixture into small balls of differing sizes (in other words I'm not too fussed whether they are all the same size). When finished, pop them all into the tomato sauce and cook them for 6 minutes before adding the cherry tomatoes, chopped coriander, baby spinach, sugar and nam pla. Cook for a further 4 minutes, check the seasoning and serve.

Pan-fried tuna steaks with soy pak choi

Per serving
259 cals
7.4g fat
1.8g saturates
6.1g sugar

1.4g fibre
2.9g salt

2.4g fat per 100g

Fresh tuna is classified as an oil-rich fish, so contains good amounts of omega-3 fats. Plus, it's packed with protein.

Serves 4

60ml Japanese soy sauce
60ml mirin
60ml sake
2 teaspoons liquid honey
1 teaspoon grated ginger
juice of 1 lime
4 x 150g tuna steaks
spray of vegetable oil
8 small heads pak choi, halved
4 spring onions, finely sliced
1 long red chilli, deseeded and sliced

Combine the soy sauce, mirin, sake, honey, ginger and lime juice in a bowl, and stir well to combine. Marinate the tuna in this mixture for 40 minutes.

Spray a griddle pan with vegetable oil and place over a medium heat. Drain the tuna (reserving the marinade) and cook for 2 minutes each side, then remove and leave to rest in a warm place.

Meanwhile, in a saucepan, bring the marinade to the boil. Add the pak choi and cook over a medium heat, turning regularly. It only needs to wilt so 1½–2 minutes should be sufficient.

Place the greens on four warmed plates, top with the tuna steaks and scatter with spring onion and chilli. Serve immediately with boiled rice.

Per serving
157cals
3.8g fat
1.1g saturates
8g sugar

2.4g fibre
3.8g salt

0.8g fat per 100g

Jamaican prawn pepper pot

Serves 6

1 onion, finely chopped
1 teaspoon crushed garlic
pinch of chilli flakes
1 tablespoon olive oil
2 red peppers, deseeded and chopped
1 Scotch Bonnet chilli, left whole
2 bay leaves
2 sprigs thyme
½ teaspoon ground allspice
1.5 litres fish or chicken stock
1 sweet potato, peeled and diced
40g long-grain rice
1 courgette, finely diced
175g peeled raw tiger prawns, sliced
1 tablespoon anchovy essence
2 teaspoons tomato purée
1 x 400g tin calaloo

Place the onion, garlic and chilli in a large saucepan with the oil and cook gently for 10 minutes, until the onion has softened.

Add the peppers, whole chilli, bay leaves, thyme and allspice and stir to combine. Cook for 3 minutes.

Add the stock, sweet potato and rice and bring to the boil, then reduce the heat and simmer for 10 minutes. Stir in the courgette, prawns, anchovy essence and tomato purée and cook for another 3 minutes, before finally adding the calaloo. Fish out the Scotch Bonnet, which is very hot, when you feel the dish has reached the desired chilli heat.

Check the seasoning and serve piping hot.

Tip

I'm a fan of calaloo, the west Indian green vegetable which is increasingly available in supermarkets, but if you can't find it use defrosted frozen leaf spinach.

Tuna 'olives' with fruits

When I say 'olives' I refer to that famous dish 'Beef Olives' and here I'm treating tuna like a piece of meat but with the advantage that it cooks very quickly. The flavours involved here have a north African influence. And tuna, as we know, provides us with omega-3 fatty acids and is a great protein-rich food.

Serves 4

1 tablespoon olive oil

1 small red onion, finely diced

1 garlic clove, finely chopped

1 pinch chilli flakes

2 teaspoons harissa

25g sultanas

4 dried apricots

2 teaspoons roasted pine nuts

¼ teaspoon ground cinnamon

1 tablespoon roughly chopped coriander

85g fresh white breadcrumbs

4 x 115g tuna steaks

spray of olive oil

120ml Dry Martini

2 teaspoons snipped chives

FOR THE SALAD:

4 tomatoes, deseeded and diced

½ cucumber, deseeded and diced

½ red onion, finely diced

½ teaspoon toasted cumin

1 teaspoon chopped mint

2 tablespoons 0% fat-free yogurt

1 tablespoon lemon juice

Heat the oil in a large frying pan and cook the onion over a medium heat for 6–8 minutes until soft but not coloured. Add the garlic, chilli, harissa, sultanas, apricots and pine nuts and cook for a further 3 minutes, stirring continuously. Allow to cool.

Mix the onion with the cinnamon, coriander and breadcrumbs, season well and squeeze together to combine.

Place each tuna steak between two sheets of clingfilm and beat gently with a meat mallet or rolling pin until you have doubled the size of the fish – be careful not to rip the flesh. Season well.

Take a quarter of the bread stuffing and squeeze it into a sausage shape, place it on an edge of the tuna and roll up, securing with a cocktail stick. Repeat with the other three tuna steaks. Don't worry if some of the filling falls out, you can always push it back in with a teaspoon or your fingers.

Meanwhile make the salad, mixing together everything except the yogurt and lemon juice, which you fold in just before serving, and season.

Heat a frying pan until almost smoking, spray a fine mist of olive oil over the tuna olives and place them in the frying pan. Cook for 2–3 minutes, turning regularly, then add the Martini, letting it bubble vigorously for a minute.

Fold the yogurt and lemon juice into the salad and serve alongside the tuna.

Tip

This dish would also be great served with the Vegetable tagine (see page 164).

Squid and chickpea stew

Per serving
303 cals
7.4g fat
1.2g saturates
12.2g sugar

5.5g fibre
1g salt

1.6g fat per 100g

There's something very moreish about a comforting stew and this fishy number ticks all the boxes. When cooking squid, you're looking for that vital point between tender and rubber. You either flash-fry in seconds or stew for a lengthy period of time, and here I've chosen the second option. Serve the stew with rice or new potatoes.

Serves 4

2 teaspoons ground cumin

1 teaspoon ground coriander

1 teaspoon ground fennel

½ teaspoon ground cayenne pepper

½ teaspoon ground allspice

1 tablespoon plain flour

450g squid, cleaned and cut into bite-sized pieces

1 tablespoon olive oil

2 red onions, each cut into 6 wedges

4 garlic cloves, crushed to a paste with a little salt

1 carrot, peeled and cut into 1cm dice

1 red pepper, deseeded and cut into 1cm dice

sprig of thyme

2 bay leaves

1 tablespoon anchovy essence or sauce

180ml dry white wine

1 x 400g tin chopped tomatoes

2 teaspoons harissa

1 x 400g tin chickpeas, drained and rinsed

3 tablespoons roughly chopped parsley

In a plastic bag, shake together the spices and flour, then add the squid pieces and toss to combine. Remove the squid and shake off any excess flour.

Heat the oil in a large saucepan until very hot, then add the squid pieces and fry for 3–4 minutes, turning regularly, until brown. Add the onions, garlic, carrot, red pepper, thyme and bay leaves, reduce the heat, and cook for 6–8 minutes until the onion has started to soften.

Add the anchovy essence, wine, tomatoes and harissa and bring to the boil. Reduce the heat then cover with a lid and simmer gently for 1 hour, stirring from time to time. Test the squid to see whether it is tender; if not, cook until it's done.

Fold in the chickpeas and parsley and season to taste. Cook for 3–5 minutes to heat through.

Tip

When cutting up the squid, make the pieces on the large side as it does tend to shrink during cooking.

Grilled chilli squid

Per serving

143 cals	0.6g fibre
5.3g fat	0.7g salt
1g saturates	
1.9g sugar	**2.8g fat per 100g**

This is a very simple dish once you've mastered the art of preparing squid, but the answer to that is to get your fishmonger to do it for you. Please don't buy frozen squid as they tend to be pumped up with water and won't grill well; fresh is definitely best. Serve with steamed new potatoes and salad.

Serves 4

2 roasted red peppers from a jar,
    drained well and patted dry
2 red chillies, seeds and stem removed
½ teaspoon dried chilli flakes
½ teaspoon smoked paprika
1 teaspoon thyme leaves
2 garlic cloves, roughly chopped
2 spring onions, roughly sliced
½ bunch of coriander, leaves and stalks
1 tablespoon olive oil
500g cleaned squid
spray of vegetable oil

Place all the ingredients, apart from the squid, in a food-processor and blend until smooth. Place in a bowl.

Cut open the squid tubes and give them a quick rinse, then pat dry. Lay the squid flat on your work surface, with the inside facing up. Then, with a sharp knife, cut three-quarters through the flesh in a tight, cross-hatch effect; this helps to keep the squid tender and also looks cute when it's cooked. Cut each tube into three.

Place the squid in the red pepper marinade and leave for 30 minutes.

Spray a little oil into a griddle pan and get the pan really hot. In batches, place the squid cut side down on the hot pan and cook for 45 seconds on each side. When you turn the squid over, the pieces will roll up into tubes.

Serve immediately.

Per serving

145 cals	0g fibre
2g fat	0.2g salt
0.4g saturates	
0.7g sugar	**1g fat per 100g**

Spiced-up monkfish

This is a great way to put more flavour into a meaty fish; the marinade is certainly not for the faint-hearted or for delicate fish. Serve the monkfish with salad or the fruity Low-fat jewelled couscous on page 216.

Serves 4

1 tablespoon sweet paprika
1 teaspoon ground cumin
1 teaspoon ground coriander
½ teaspoon garam masala
½ teaspoon ground black pepper
½ teaspoon ground turmeric
60ml rice vinegar
2 tablespoons harissa
1 teaspoon garlic purée
1 teaspoon ginger purée
4 x 175g monkfish steaks
spray of vegetable oil

Combine the first ten ingredients in a bowl then spread the marinade over the fish. Leave for 3 hours for the flavour to develop.

Spray vegetable oil into a large frying pan and cook the monkfish for 5 minutes each side.

A casserole of sweet potatoes, spinach and sweet peppers

Per serving

204 cals	7.1g fibre
2.8g fat	0.5g salt
0.4g saturates	
12.8g sugar	**0.8g fat per 100g**

A lovely vegetarian stew with a few superfoods enhanced by great depth of flavour. I love the sweet potatoes, but obviously you can add whatever vegetables you like, as long as you start with the suggested onion and spice base.

Serves 4

2 teaspoons rapeseed oil

1 red onion, cut into 8 wedges

3 garlic cloves, roughly chopped

2 long red chillies, deseeded and finely sliced

1 teaspoon sweet paprika

½ teaspoon ground cumin

½ teaspoon ground fennel

2 sweet potatoes, peeled and cut into
   8 wedges each

8 pepperdew peppers, drained and halved

1 x 400g tin chopped tomatoes

1 x 400g tin cannellini beans

2 tablespoons chopped parsley

2 handfuls baby leaf spinach, washed

2 tablespoons 0% fat Greek yogurt

Heat the oil in a large saucepan, then add the onion, garlic and chilli and cook over a medium heat for 8–10 minutes to soften but not colour the onions.

Stir in the spices, then add the sweet potato, peppers and tinned tomatoes. Cook, uncovered, for 20 minutes, stirring from time to time. Season.

Fold in the cannellini beans, parsley and spinach and cook for about 5 minutes until the beans are hot and the spinach has wilted. (You will have to be careful when adding the spinach as it can easily end up over your cooker…fold it in carefully!)

Serve in four warm bowls and top with a little yogurt.

Red snapper with roast cherry tomatoes, garlic and basil

Per serving

213 cals	1.5g fibre
5.6g fat	0.8g salt
1.1g saturates	
3.9g sugar	**1.8g fat per 100g**

I'm a converted fan of red snapper, especially the variety known as Bourgeois, but have come to realise that it needs big flavours as it's a really meaty fish. As with most fish, red snapper mustn't be overcooked, so this dish is perfect for a fast supper, and a delicious and healthy one, too. Serve with new potatoes.

Serves 4

250g red cherry tomatoes

250g yellow cherry tomatoes

12 garlic cloves, peeled

1 tablespoon olive oil

4 x 175g snapper fillets, skin on, cut
   into 2.5cm dice

1 tablespoon Lilliput capers, drained

1 tablespoon sherry vinegar

16 basil leaves, ripped

Preheat the oven to 190°C/gas mark 5.

Put the tomatoes, garlic and olive oil in a bowl, season with salt and pepper and toss to coat. Tip into a roasting tray, place in the oven and cook for 25 minutes, stirring from time to time.

Add the fish pieces, season and cook for a further 10–12 minutes before adding capers, vinegar and basil leaves. Toss gently to combine and wilt the basil leaves, taking care not to break up the fish.

I love noodles

Per serving

366 cals	5.7g fibre
9.2g fat	1.7g salt
0.8g saturates	
10.8g sugar	**1.9g fat per 100g**

I say 'I love noodles' rather than describe it as 'pork noodles' because this is a one-fits-all dish: you could substitute beef fillet, chicken breast, prawns or squid as the main source of protein. And, as a bonus, you'll find this will be a winner with all the family.

Serves 4

450g fresh egg noodles
spray of vegetable oil
300g pork fillet (tenderloin), trimmed
    and shaved very thinly
2 teaspoons vegetable oil
4 spring onions, sliced on the diagonal
1 green pepper, deseeded and cut into
    2.5cm pieces
1 carrot, peeled and shaved into long
    peelings with a potato peeler
1 courgette, shaved into long peelings
    with a potato peeler
115g button mushrooms, cleaned
    and quartered
2 garlic cloves, thinly sliced
1 teaspoon grated ginger
½ teaspoon Sichuan ground pepper
2 tablespoons oyster sauce
2 tablespoons reduced-salt soy sauce
2 teaspoons grated palm sugar or
    liquid honey
175g sugar snaps or mange tout
3 pak choi, cut in half

Pour boiling water over the noodles to cover and leave for 1 minute. Then, without burning your fingers, separate the noodles, drain and set aside to keep warm.

Over a very high heat, warm a wok until smoking before spraying with oil then quickly and in batches pan-fry the pork fillet until brown, about 2 minutes. Remove and set aside to keep warm.

Add the oil to the wok, heat to high, then stir-fry the onions, green pepper and carrot for 2 minutes. Add 2 tablespoons water, followed by the courgette, mushrooms, garlic, ginger and pepper, and cook for a further minute.

Add the oyster sauce, soy sauce, palm sugar or honey, sugar snaps, and pak choi, along with the noodles and pork. Toss for about 2 minutes until the pak choi has wilted and the noodles and pork warmed through.

Serve in four warm bowls.

Sweet and not-so-sour chicken

Per serving

204 cals   2.7g fibre

6.9g fat   2.5g salt

1g saturates

13.1g sugar   **2g fat per 100g**

This is a really easy and exceptionally delicious chicken dish that should please the whole family. Don't be tempted to use tinned pineapple – it just won't be good enough and you'll miss out on the crunch of fresh.

Serves 4

2 tablespoons vegetable oil

1 onion, thinly sliced

3 garlic cloves, thinly sliced

2 skinless, boneless chicken breasts, each cut into thin slivers

1 red pepper, deseeded and cut into 2.5cm pieces

1 tablespoon fish sauce

2 tablespoons oyster sauce

2 tablespoons tomato ketchup

2 x 2cm slices of pineapple, peeled, cored and cut into 2cm cubes

3 ripe tomatoes, each roughly cut into about six pieces

½ cucumber, peeled, deseeded and cut into 2cm cubes

1 tablespoon reduced-salt soy sauce

8 mint leaves, shredded

Heat a wok, add the oil and cook the onion and garlic over a high heat for 3–4 minutes, stirring constantly, until the onions start to brown.

Add the chicken slivers and red peppers and cook for 2 minutes, stirring continuously. Add the three sauces, together with the pineapple, tomatoes and cucumber. Toss vigorously to combine and cook for 2 minutes.

Season with soy sauce, garnish with mint and serve with rice.

Tip

'What do I do with the rest of the pineapple?' I hear you say. Grilled pineapple slices with honey and fresh lime would be my suggestion.

Vietnamese beef and noodles

Per serving

306 cals	2.3g fibre
5.7g fat	0.9g salt
2.4g saturates	
3.3g sugar	**0.8g fat per 100g**

I would hate to upset the Vietnamese with their iconoclastic beef dish Pho Bo, but mine is 'loosely' based on this classic. On a low-fat diet we can't eat a lot of beef, but this one passes muster. It's a great way to eat – soupy, noodley, beefy.

Serves 4

1.2 litres beef stock, home-made
    if possible
600ml water
1 stalk of lemongrass, left whole,
    bruised
2 Thai red chillies, left whole
2 lime leaves
4 garlic cloves, smashed
bunch of coriander, stalks and leaves
1 star anise
10cm piece of root ginger, thinly sliced
325g beef fillet, trimmed and thinly
    sliced
spray of oil
175g dried thin vermicelli rice noodles
115g mangetout, thinly sliced
    lengthways
12 button mushrooms, quartered
2 pak choi, roughly cut
16 mint leaves, shredded
2 tablespoons lime juice
1 tablespoon fish sauce
85g beansprouts
6 spring onions, finely sliced
thinly sliced red chillies and lime
    wedges, to serve

In a large pot, heat the beef stock and water with the lemongrass, chillies, lime leaves, garlic and coriander stalks, star anise and ginger. Bring to the boil, reduce the heat and simmer for 20 minutes. Strain, discarding the solids, and return to the saucepan.

Heat a large frying pan. Season the beef, spray with a light misting of oil and pan-fry over a high heat for about 45 seconds each side. Set aside to keep warm.

Pour boiling water over the noodles, leave to soften for about 1 minute, then drain and divide between four warm bowls.

Meanwhile, add the mangetout, mushrooms, pak choi, mint and coriander leaves to the broth and cook for 1 minute. Stir in the lime juice and fish sauce.

Scatter the beansprouts and spring onions over the noodles and top with slices of beef then spoon on the vegetable broth. Serve with extra chilli and lime wedges.

Peppered chicken with tomatoes and courgettes

Per serving
168 cals   3g fibre
4.8g fat   0.2g salt
1g saturates
8.9g sugar   **1.3g fat per 100g**

This is another very simple chicken dish, concentrating on big flavour – this time it's pepper, with a glancing visit to India. It's an all-in-one dish, although you may want to serve it with rice or new potatoes.

Serves 4

8 skinless, boneless chicken thighs, cut into 3
2 teaspoons vegetable oil
2 teaspoons freshly ground black pepper
4 garlic cloves, finely chopped
1 teaspoon grated ginger root
2 onions, cut into wedges
4 tomatoes, roughly chopped
1 teaspoon ground turmeric
1 teaspoon garam masala
2 large courgettes, cut into 2cm rings
approx 120ml water
3 tablespoons chopped coriander

Toss the chicken thigh meat in the oil, then coat in half the pepper and season with salt.

Heat a saucepan and cook the chicken gently to colour but not scorch (spices become bitter if the heat is too intense). Brown all over, then remove the chicken and set aside.

Add the garlic, ginger and onions to the pan and fry over a medium heat for 8–10 minutes to lightly colour and soften the onion. Add the remaining black pepper, tomatoes, turmeric, garam masala, courgettes and the water. Cook for 5 minutes, then return the chicken to the pan and cook for 10 minutes longer, before checking the seasoning and folding in the coriander.

Tip

If your tomatoes are a fairly tasteless variety, you might do better to add a 400g tin of chopped tomatoes, in which case you won't need the water.

Fast and furious prawns

I say 'furious', because you're getting a chilli whammy. They are delicious hot or cold – served with a salad, for example, or slapped between slices of bread. I'll sometimes have them ready in the fridge to be picked at from time to time.

Serves 4

32 raw tiger prawns, peeled
½ teaspoon salt
juice of 1 lemon
1 teaspoon grated ginger
1 teaspoon grated garlic
½ teaspoon dried chilli flakes
spray of vegetable oil
grated zest of 1 orange
2 tablespoons coriander, chopped
1 teaspoon mint, chopped

Combine the prawns with the salt and lemon in a bowl and leave for 20 minutes; this cleans the prawns and starts the 'cooking' process by marination.

Rinse and dry the prawns, then mix with the ginger, garlic and chilli. Spray with oil, mixing the prawns well to make sure that they are all evenly coated.

Heat a frying pan over a high heat. Tip in the prawns and cook for 1–2 minutes each side until they've turned pink. Toss with the orange, coriander and mint, and serve immediately.

Roast onions with curried crab

My sort of food takes a little effort. So, with a little effort here you end up with a creatively different main course.

Serves 4

4 large onions, unpeeled
2 teaspoons vegetable oil
1 hot red chilli, finely diced
1 tablespoon Thai red curry paste
1 tablespoon smooth mango chutney
225g cooked long-grain rice
175g fresh or canned white crabmeat,
  flaked
2 tablespoons 0% fat Greek yogurt
1 tablespoon chopped coriander
1 tablespoon lime juice
1 tablespoon fish sauce

Place the onions, unpeeled and uncut, in a deep saucepan of salted water. Bring to the boil, reduce the heat then simmer for 15–20 minutes. Remove and set aside until cool enough to handle.

Peel the onions, and cut a very shallow section off the root end to crease a flat base. Cut one-fifth off the top of each onion and, with a teaspoon or melon baller, scoop out the centre of each onion leaving at least two layers of onion on the outside to create the casing.

Preheat the oven to 180°C/gas mark 4.

Chop half the onion centres finely and place in a frying pan with the oil. Cook gently for 6–8 minutes then add the chilli and curry paste and cook until fragrant, about 2 minutes. Add the chutney and rice and stir to combine. Remove from the heat and stir in the crab, yogurt, coriander, lime juice and fish sauce.

Fill the onions with this mixture and place the tray in the oven and cook for 25–30 minutes until bubbling.

Serve with purple sprouting broccoli and new potatoes.

Fruit and fibre chicken

Per serving
404 cals   2.6g fibre
3.5g fat   1g salt
0.6g saturates
29.7g sugar   **1.2g fat per 100g**

As we're not allowed to eat chicken skin the question arises as to how to stop the flesh going leathery without the skin's protection? We need a crust but not just any crust, we need a crust with flavour, so here it is. Serve with new potatoes, mustard and your favourite green vegetable.

Serves 4

25g porridge oats
2 teaspoons very finely chopped rosemary
grated zest of 1 orange
25g dried cranberries, finely chopped
120ml 0% fat Greek yogurt
2 teaspoons wholegrain Dijon-style
   mustard
1 egg white, beaten
4 x 175g skinless, boneless chicken breasts
55g seasoned flour
spray of olive oil

FILLING:

8 dried apricots
orange juice, for soaking
25g plump sultanas
25g dried cherries
25g dried blueberries

Cut open each apricot to create a cavity, then cover with orange juice. Put the sultanas, cherries and blueberries to soak in orange juice in another bowl. Leave all the fruit to soak for 1 hour.

Combine the porridge oats, rosemary, orange zest and chopped cranberries in one bowl and beat together the yogurt, mustard and egg white in another.

Place the chicken breasts on a chopping board and make a deep incision through the side of each breast leaving the ends intact so you create deep pockets.

Mix together the drained sultanas, cherries and blueberries and use to stuff the apricot cavities. Push two filled apricots into the deep cut of each chicken breast, also pushing in any leftover berries.

Carefully roll the chicken breasts in the seasoned flour, then in the yogurt mixture, making sure that the coating has stuck to the flour, then finally roll the chicken in the oats. Refrigerate until ready to use.

Preheat the oven to 180°C/gas mark 4.

Spray the chicken in a fine mist of olive oil, place on a rack over a roasting tray and bake in the oven for 35 minutes. Season and serve.

Chicken in a pot

Per serving

269 cals	4.7g fibre
5g fat	1.1g salt
1.2g saturates	
11.5g sugar	**1g fat per 100g**

Now I would love to pot roast a whole chicken and I could ask you to remove the skin before carving, but would you? The skin also produces quite a lot of liquid fat during the cooking process which you would have to skim off. This is all starting to sound like too much hassle, so skinless thighs it will be; these retain their moisture more than breasts, but if you prefer to use chicken breasts, feel free to substitute one small breast for every two thighs.

Serves 6

2 onions, roughly chopped

2 carrots, peeled and roughly chopped

2 sticks of celery, cut thinly

1 head of garlic, halved horizontally

2 teaspoons olive oil

3 sprigs of thyme

3 bay leaves

1 x 400g tin chopped tomatoes

300ml dry white wine

12 chicken thighs

300ml chicken stock

250g fresh penne pasta

115g frozen petits pois, defrosted

1 courgette, cut into pea-sized dice

Preheat the oven to 180°C/gas 4.

In an ovenproof, lidded, casserole dish, cook the onion, carrot, celery and garlic in the oil over a medium heat for about 8–10 minutes, until the onion starts to soften.

Add the thyme, bay leaves, tomatoes and wine and bring to the boil. Nestle the chicken thighs into the vegetables and add enough stock to make sure that everything is covered. Cover with the lid and cook in the oven for 40 minutes.

Remove the chicken thighs to keep warm, then place the casserole on the hob over a high heat. Add any remaining stock and bring to the boil.

Tip in the fresh pasta, peas and courgettes and stir to combine. Cook for 3 minutes, stirring regularly. Return the chicken to the pot and warm through. Serve with some crusty bread.

Tip

If you don't have any fresh pasta, use dried but extend the cooking time accordingly.

Chicken and prawn risotto

Per serving

482 cals	2.3g fibre
8.6g fat	3.4g salt
2.1g saturates	
4.3g sugar	**1.3g fat per 100g**

Risotto is about the rice. Too often in non-Italian countries there's a habit of putting in far too many other ingredients, making the finished dish very heavy. Once you've mastered the slow addition of liquid, you are at liberty to experiment with the content. Risotto is often finished off with butter and Parmesan, which are low-fat no-nos, hence the addition of yogurt towards the end.

Serves 4

750ml chicken stock

750ml water

1 tablespoon olive oil

1 onion, finely diced

2 garlic cloves, crushed to a paste with a little salt

4 sage leaves, finely chopped

1 stick celery, finely diced

4 skinless boneless chicken thighs, each cut in 3

325g Arborio rice

16 raw tiger prawns

spray of olive oil

115g frozen petit pois, defrosted

2 tablespoons 0% fat Greek style yogurt

2 tablespoons chopped parsley

In a large saucepan, heat together the stock and water until boiling, then reduce the heat and keep it at a simmer.

In another large, non-stick saucepan, heat the oil then cook the onion over a medium heat for 8 minutes before adding the garlic, sage, celery and chicken. Cook for a further 3 minutes, gently colouring the chicken.

Add the rice, stir to combine and cook for a couple of minutes until the rice turns opaque and releases a nutty smell.

Add one ladle of hot stock and stir constantly until most of the liquor has evaporated, then add another ladle and repeat. The heat should be reasonably aggressive, hence the reason for stirring. Carry on in this way until the rice is tender but still a tad al dente, about 18–20 minutes. You may well not need all the stock.

Towards the end of the risotto cooking time, heat a frying pan, spray the prawns with some oil and pan-fry over a high heat until pink all over. Add to the risotto, along with the peas, yogurt and parsley. Stir to combine, season and serve in four warm bowls.

Tip

As the rice cooks, it releases starch into the liquid creating a creamy emulsion. Risotto should not be dry – it should be a little soupy, giving slightly when spooned into the bowl.

Turkey chow mein

Per serving
440 cals
12.4g fat
3.5g saturates
11.1g sugar

7.2g fibre
4.3g salt

2.3g fat per 100g

If you want to get the children to eat more healthily, then I'm afraid you may have to pander to their tastes, but don't worry because actually, made well, this dish appeals to everyone. In many ways it's better than having it at your local Chinese, where the odd sprinkle of MSG tends to slip in.

Serves 4

2 teaspoons sesame oil

2 onions, finely chopped

1 carrot, peeled and finely chopped

1 green pepper, seeded and cut in 1cm dice

2 garlic cloves, finely chopped

1 medium red chilli, thinly sliced

325g lean turkey or chicken mince

1 tablespoon mild curry paste (Indian)

115g shiitake mushrooms, stalks removed and discarded, caps finely sliced

180ml chicken stock

90ml oyster sauce

30ml light reduced-salt soy sauce

450g fresh thin egg noodles

85g frozen petits pois, defrosted

2 pak choi, shredded

Heat the oil in a large wok, add the onion, carrot, green pepper, garlic, chilli and mince and cook over a medium heat until the mince is golden, about 10 minutes. Break up any clods of mince with the back of a wooden spoon as it cooks.

Add the curry paste and mushrooms and stir to combine, cooking for 2 minutes before adding the stock and oyster and soy sauces.

Cook until boiling, then fold in the noodles, peas and pak choi and cook for 2 minutes. Check the seasoning and serve really hot.

Tip

Pork or beef mince could also be substituted for the turkey.

An Italian lamb feast

Per serving
456 cals
10.6g fat
3.5g saturates
12.2g sugar

5.6g fibre
0.5g salt

1.9g fat per 100g

This dish is a great alternative to a Sunday roast, though there's none of your pink lamb here. This is falling-off-the-bone-style cooking, which involves a little work towards the end of cooking, skimming off the fat, but is full of flavour.

Serves 6

1 small leg of lamb on the bone
   (ideally no bigger than 1kg)
2 garlic cloves, half sliced and half
   finely chopped
½ bunch of fresh oregano or marjoram
2 onions, finely chopped
2 teaspoons olive oil
½ butternut squash, peeled, deseeded
   and cut into 3cm pieces
1 x 400g tin cherry tomatoes
1 x 400g tin chopped tomatoes
1 tablespoon Greek or wild dried
   oregano
325g dried macaroni (small)
1 tablespoon Lilliput (baby) capers,
   drained
2 tablespoons chopped parsley

Preheat the oven to 150°C/gas mark 2.

Make several slashes or deep holes all over the lamb and insert a slice of garlic and a small sprig of oregano or marjoram into each cut. Season with salt and ground black pepper.

Place the onion, oil and butternut squash in a bowl and toss together, then place in a roasting tray big enough to take the lamb. Pour in the two types of tomatoes and the dried oregano, and stir to combine.

Place the lamb on top and cook for 2½ hours. Pour a glass of water in every so often as the liquids in the base dry out, and baste the lamb with the juices.

After the allotted time, remove the lamb to rest and keep warm, then pour the remains of the pan into a heatproof glass jug and leave to stand for 5 minutes to allow the fat to separate from the juice. Skim off the fat then tip the contents of the jug into a saucepan. Add enough boiling water to provide sufficient liquid to cook the pasta, then add the macaroni. Cook for 1 minute longer than suggested in the manufacturer's instructions.

Fold in the capers and parsley, season to taste, then pour the pasta sauce over the lamb.

Tip

Any leftovers will make for a delicious meal later in the week, when the flavours have intensified over time.

Turkey, spinach and courgette lasagne

Per serving

382 cals	5.4g fibre
7.7g fat	1.5g salt
1.9g saturates	
14.8g sugar	**1.3g fat per 100g**

Everybody seems to enjoy lasagne but classically it's very high in fat, so I've reduced this by using less cheese and making a white sauce with cornflour instead of the normal roux made with butter and flour.

Serves 6–8

450ml skimmed milk

1 onion, halved

2 bay leaves

1 stick of celery

½ teaspoon ground nutmeg

1½ tablespoons cornflour, loosened to a paste with a little water

325g frozen chopped spinach pellets, defrosted

225g turkey escalopes, beaten thinly

8 sheets of lasagne verde

2 courgettes, thinly sliced lengthways

115g low-fat cottage cheese

2 tablespoons grated Parmesan

SAUCE:

1 onion, finely chopped

1 tablespoon olive oil

2 garlic cloves, crushed to a paste with a little salt

2 anchovy fillets, roughly chopped

1 teaspoon dried oregano

12 stoned Kalamata black olives, roughly chopped

1 x 400g tin chopped tomatoes

2 teaspoons tomato purée

Preheat the oven to 200°C/gas mark 6.

To make the tomato sauce, cook the onion in a large saucepan with the oil over a medium to low heat for 8–10 minutes until softened but not coloured. Add the garlic, anchovy and oregano and cook for a further 4 minutes until the anchovy breaks down. Add the olives, tomatoes and purée and cook for 15 minutes until thick. Season and set aside.

Meanwhile, put the milk in a pan with the onion, bay, celery and nutmeg and bring to the boil. Simmer for 15 minutes to infuse the flavours, then strain and return to the boil. Stir in the cornflour paste and cook for 2–3 minutes to thicken, and check the seasoning.

Squeeze the spinach as dry as possible then mix it with about a third of the white sauce. Spoon half the spinach mixture into the base of an ovenproof baking dish. Lay the turkey escalopes over the spinach then spoon half the tomato sauce over the turkey. Lay on four lasagne sheets then top with the remaining spinach. Next lay on the courgette slices, another four sheets of lasagne followed by the remaining tomato sauce.

Pour over the white sauce, mixing it a little with the tomato sauce. Dot over the cottage cheese then sprinkle with Parmesan.

Cook in the oven for 45 minutes from cold or 30 minutes if you're doing it immediately after construction.

Turkey ragout

Per serving

309 cals   2.9g fibre
10.3g fat   1.4g salt
4.1g saturates
10.2g sugar   **2.5g fat per 100g**

A good ragout or bolognaise sauce is a useful standby for freezing, as you can use it for pasta, as a filling for shepherd's pie, or as a base for a moussaka or (cheese-free) lasagne. The chicken liver is barely noticeable when the mince has finished cooking, but it adds a great depth of flavour.

Serves 6

1 tablespoon olive oil
2 onions, finely diced
3 garlic cloves, crushed to a paste
   with a little salt
1 stick of celery, finely sliced
2 carrots, peeled and diced
2 bay leaves
2 tablespoons dried oregano
½ teaspoon dried chilli flakes
675g turkey or chicken mince
175g chicken livers, chopped (optional)
175ml red wine
1 x 400g tin chopped tomatoes
300ml chicken stock
1 tablespoon Worcestershire sauce

Put half the olive oil in a large saucepan, followed by the onions, garlic, celery, carrots, bay leaves, oregano and chilli, and cook for 8–10 minutes over a medium heat, stirring regularly.

Add the remaining oil to a large frying pan and, over a high heat, cook the mince and chicken livers, if using, until golden brown, breaking up any lumps with the back of a wooden spoon. Add to the vegetables.

Pour the wine into the empty frying pan and bring to the boil, scraping up any caramelised residue that has stuck to the bottom. Add to the ragout mixture.

Finally, add the chopped tomatoes, stock and Worcestershire sauce, and bring to the boil, stirring regularly. Reduce the heat and simmer, covered, for at least 1½ hours. For the last 20 minutes, remove the lid to allow the mixture to thicken and reduce. Season and serve with pasta, rice or any of the suggestions above.

Tip

If you allow the mixture to cool and then refrigerate it, you can then scoop off any fat that is sitting on the surface.

Bass in an Asian bag

Per serving

257 cals   2.8g fibre
5.6g fat   0.9g salt
1g saturates
2.3g sugar   **1.9g fat per 100g**

Cooking 'en papillote' – the French name for this form of cookery – has slipped out of fashion for no particular reason other than laziness, and yet it is so simple and seals in so much flavour.

Serves 4

1 teaspoon sesame oil
4 x 175g fillets of sea bass, scaled and
   pin-boned
1 teaspoon grated ginger
½ teaspoon grated garlic
1 medium-heat red chilli, deseeded and sliced
4 spring onions, thinly sliced on the diagonal
1 x 400g tin butter beans, drained and rinsed
1½ tablespoons reduced-salt soy sauce
2 tablespoons sake, mirin or dry sherry
8 cherry tomatoes, halved

Preheat the oven to 200°C/gas mark 6.

Rub the sesame oil over the sea bass fillets, top and bottom, then lay each one, skin side down, on a large rectangle of foil or baking parchment.

Combine the ginger, garlic, chilli and half the spring onions and sprinkle over the fish, then scatter around the butter beans.

Gather up the foil sides a little but before you seal the parcel, pour in the soy sauce and sake and top with the cherry tomatoes. Seal the parcels tightly and place on a baking tray, then cook for 15 minutes.

Remove from the oven and allow to sit for 5 minutes. Open the parcel slightly and scatter with the remaining spring onion slices.

Penne puttanesca

Per serving

447 cals   6.6g fibre
6.9g fat   2.3g salt
1g saturates
8.7g sugar   **1.2g fat per 100g**

I've added extra chilli to this classic pasta dish, but feel free to omit or increase the heat, and I've also had to drastically reduce the amount of oil. But please don't swamp your pasta with sauce: the Italians use just a little sauce to coat the pasta whereas we Brits tend to have a little pasta to go with the sauce.

Serves 4

3 garlic cloves, finely chopped
4 anchovy fillets, drained and patted dry
2 tablespoons Lilliput (baby) capers
2 teaspoons extra virgin olive oil
4 dried chillies, left whole
2 onions, finely chopped
1 teaspoon dried oregano
1 x 400g tin chopped tomatoes
85g Kalamata olives, stoned and chopped
120ml water
400g dried penne

Put a deep pan of heavily salted water on to boil for the pasta.

In a large saucepan, cook the garlic, anchovy and capers gently in the oil until the anchovies have broken down.

Add the chillies, onions and oregano and cook gently for 8 minutes, then add the tomatoes, olives and water. Bring to the boil, reduce the heat and simmer until the sauce is dark and thick. Keep tasting the sauce as it cooks and, when it reaches the desired degree of chilli heat, fish out the chillies.

Towards the end of the cooking time, boil the penne for about 1 minute less than it says on the manufacturer's instructions. Drain and, with the water still clinging to it, tip the pasta immediately into the sauce. Stir to combine and serve immediately.

Aromatic vegetable parcel

Per serving

110 cals   4.7g fibre
0.7g fat   0.5g salt
0.1g saturates
12.9g sugar   **0.2g fat per 100g**

When you're on one diet or another, it's vital to add a little inspiration to what will often be a dull menu. This dish is an exciting way to serve a lovely combination of different vegetables.

Serves 4

½ butternut squash, deseeded and
    cut into 2cm chunks
2 celery hearts, cut in 4 lengthways
    and washed thoroughly
1 red pepper, deseeded and cut
    into strips
4 cocktail or pickling onions
4 radishes, topped and tailed
4 whole baby courgettes
2 teaspoons chopped mint
juice and grated zest of 1 orange
120ml dry martini
½ teaspoon sweet paprika
¼ teaspoon salt
½ teaspoon freshly ground
    black pepper

Put all the vegetables in one bowl. Combine all the remaining ingredients in a separate bowl and stir well to dissolve.

Preheat the oven to 180°C/gas mark 4, unless you prefer to use a steamer (see below).

Place four large squares of baking parchment (30 x 30cm) on your work surface and divide the vegetables between the four sheets. Working on one sheet at a time, bring the sides of the parchment up together to create an open parcel then pour in a quarter of the aromatic liquid. Twist the paper edges together to seal the parcel. Repeat with the others.

Either cook the parcels in the oven for 35 minutes or the steamer for 25 minutes, until the vegetables are tender.

Tip

You can obviously use different vegetables, but try to choose vegetables that will take the same time to cook. The citrus juices can be changed to lime and lemon and the mint to coriander or tarragon.

Beef pancakes with chilli and ginger

We can get away with using beef by using less of it and trimming off visible fat. With the addition of noodles and vegetables we can eat this beef pancake with relish.

Serves 4

2 tablespoons ginger syrup (from the stem ginger below)

2 teaspoons reduced-salt soy sauce

2 teaspoons soft dark brown sugar

1 teaspoon grated ginger

2 garlic cloves, crushed to a paste with a little salt

1 hot red chilli, finely chopped

275g fillet steaks, cut into thin strips

115g vermicelli thin rice noodles soaked in hot water for 3 minutes then refreshed and drained

spray of vegetable oil

1 leek, washed and cut into thin julienne strips

1 carrot, peeled and cut into julienne strips

4 shop-bought savoury pancakes

¼ pineapple, peeled and cored and cut into thin strips

1 tablespoon chopped coriander

3 spring onions, thinly sliced

1 x 2cm piece stem ginger, cut into julienne strips

In a bowl, combine the ginger syrup with the soy sauce, brown sugar, grated ginger, garlic and chilli. Stir to combine. Place the beef in a shallow tray, pour the marinade over and leave to marinate for 2 hours.

Prepare the noodles by soaking them in hot water for 3 minutes then refresh and drain them.

Spray a frying pan with vegetable oil and place over a high heat. Cook the marinated steak for 2 minutes, remove and set aside to keep warm.

To the same pan, add the leek, carrot and noodles, together with the marinade, and cook for 2 minutes to heat through.

Warm the pancakes in the microwave then lay out on your work surface. Cover the surface of each pancake with the thin pineapple slices, then lay the beef down the centre. Top the beef with the noodle mixture, followed by a sprinkling of coriander, spring onion and stem ginger. Roll up and serve immediately.

Tip

This recipe works equally well with strips of chicken breast or diced salmon or tuna.

Salads and side orders

Fennel, ruby grapefruit and red onion salad

Per serving

55 cals	2.3g fibre
3.7g fat	0.5g salt
0.5g saturates	
4.5g sugar	**3g fat per 100g**

A classic combo that is a good source of folic acid and vitamin C. These lovely wintery flavours enhance grilled fish beautifully and I can also see it going well with a young roast partridge.

Serves 4

1 large fennel bulb, tough outside layer removed, and very thinly sliced

1 ruby grapefruit, peeled, pith removed and segments cut from between each membrane, juices from the membrane squeezed into a bowl

6 leaves from 1 Belgian endive or chicory, finely sliced

1 small red onion, finely sliced

½ teaspoon ground cumin

1 tablespoon extra virgin olive oil

6 mint leaves, finely shredded

8 Kalamata olives, stoned, in brine, rinsed and drained

salt and ground black pepper

Add all the ingredients to the grapefruit juice and toss to combine. Season to taste.

Tip

If you find the salad too bitter, add one teaspoon of runny honey to the grapefruit juice before adding the remaining ingredients.

Fennel, apple and red onion salad

Per serving

60 cals	1.6g fibre
0.7g fat	0.2g salt
0g saturates	
8.8g sugar	**0.5g fat per 100g**

A light, refreshing salad that would go well with fish.

Serves 4

2 tablespoons cider vinegar

4 tablespoons 0% fat Greek yogurt

2 teaspoons Dijon mustard

1 teaspoon brown mustard seeds, soaked in cold water for 1 hour

1 teaspoon runny honey

1 Granny Smith apple, quartered, cored and thinly sliced

1 red onion, thinly sliced

1 small fennel bulb, outside layer removed, very thinly sliced

1 tablespoon chopped dill

Place the first five ingredients in a bowl and whisk to combine.

Mix the apple, onion, fennel and dill then add enough dressing to coat. Season well.

Chilli chicken salad

Per serving
191 cals   2.8g fibre
4.4g fat   2.2g salt
1.1g saturates
8.8g sugar   **1.3g fat per 100g**

This is a salad you can make with the leftover Sunday roast chicken, but you could use cooked chicken breast or poach a couple of chicken breasts specially, too.

Serves 4

325g cooked skinless chicken, shredded
1 carrot, peeled and cut into shavings
   (use the peeler)
½ cucumber, peeled and cut into shavings,
   discarding the seeds
4 radishes, thinly sliced
1 small red pepper, cut into julienne strips
½ Chinese or ¼ Savoy cabbage, thinly
   shredded
4 spring onions, thinly sliced on the
   diagonal
40g beansprouts, soaked in iced water
1 red chilli, deseeded and thinly sliced
2 tablespoons coriander leaves
2 handfuls of rocket leaves

CHILLI DRESSING:

juice of 2 limes and grated zest of 1 lime
3 tablespoons sweet chilli sauce
1 garlic clove, crushed to a paste with
   a little salt
½ teaspoon grated ginger
1 tablespoon oyster sauce
1 teaspoon kecap manis
1 teaspoon sesame oil

Combine all the dressing ingredients in a bottle or jam jar and shake well to mix. Leave for 30 minutes for the flavours to develop.

In a bowl, mix together all the salad ingredients and coat with the dressing just before serving.

Panzanella – Italian bread and tomato salad

Per serving

154 cals   2g fibre

4.5g fat   1g salt

0.7g saturates

5.9g sugar   **2.9g fat per 100g**

Lycopene, vitamin C and beta-carotenes are all going on here. which makes this healthy salad tick all the right boxes when it comes to your wellbeing. I've reduced the oil content and upped the vinegar, softened with a little sugar.

Serves 4

1 tablespoon extra virgin olive oil

2 tablespoons red wine vinegar

½ teaspoon Tabasco sauce

2 garlic cloves, crushed to a paste
 with a little sea salt

3 tablespoons tomato juice or passata

1 teaspoon caster sugar

1 small red onion, thinly sliced

3 beefsteak tomatoes, cored and cut
 into rough small chunks

3 thick slices day-old ciabatta bread,
 broken into rough chunks

10 large basil leaves, torn

Combine the oil with the vinegar, Tabasco, garlic, tomato juice and sugar, stir to dissolve the sugar.

Add the onion, tomato and bread and stir to combine, check the seasoning, then scatter with basil. Allow the flavours to develop for 45 minutes before serving at room temperature.

Tip

If you prefer a softer texture to your bread, soak the chunks in cold water for 5 minutes, then squeeze to partially dry before adding to the salad. For a more crunchy salad, toast the bread before ripping it up and adding to the salad.

Per serving

23 cals   1.1g fibre

0.2g fat   0g salt

0.1g saturates

4.4g sugar   **0.2g fat per 100g**

A tropical savoury salad

This salad is based on the Indian 'kachumbers' – fresh, vibrant and healthy, with lots of zing.

Serves 6

¼ cucumber, peeled, deseeded and
 cut into 1cm chunks

1 small red onion, finely sliced

6 radishes, sliced

½ mango, peeled and cut into
 1cm chunks

3 tomatoes, deseeded and cut
 into 1cm dice

½ teaspoon caster sugar

1 tablespoon chopped coriander

2 teaspoons chopped mint

juice and grated zest of 1 lime

Combine all of the ingredients and serve immediately.

Tip

If you're going to prepare the salad ahead, add the herbs and lime juice just before serving.

Pomelo and pomegranate salad

Per serving
85 cals
0.6g fat
0.1g saturates
17.4g sugar

2g fibre
0.3g salt

0.3g fat per 100g

You see pomelos in the shops but you never see anyone buying them. In Thailand they separate all the juice droplets and make a fab salad but that's fairly heavy-duty stuff, so all I'm asking here is for you to cut the fruit into segments. I've moved from Thailand to further West for my influences in this dish.

Serves 4

2 large pomelos
1 red onion, finely sliced
4 spring onions, sliced
2 tablespoons chopped coriander
1 teaspoon chopped mint
¼ small white cabbage, cored and
  finely shredded
2 garlic cloves, crushed to a paste
  with a little salt
1 teaspoon rose harissa
2 teaspoons honey
1 tablespoon pomegranate molasses
3 tablespoons pomegranate seeds

Peel, remove the pith and cut between the membranes of the pomelos to create segments. Do this over a bowl to catch the juices, then after segmenting, squeeze the empty membrane to release the remaining juice. Then separate the juice from the segments.

Combine the segments with the red and spring onions, coriander, mint and cabbage in one bowl.

In the bowl which contains the pomelo juice, add the garlic, harissa, honey and molasses. Mix to combine then pour over the pomelo salad. Stir to mix well then season before sprinkling over the pomegranate seeds, serve immediately.

Tip

If pomelos are unobtainable use a combination of red grapefruit and mandarin slices, peeled of course.

Pea, corn and baby courgette salad

Per serving
86 cals
2.1g fat
0.4g saturates
8.3g sugar

2.7g fibre
0.8g salt

1.2g fat per 100g

This is a really nice mixture that doubles up as a great vegetarian garnish. The miso paste adds a lovely nutty flavour.

Serves 4

1 teaspoon vegetable oil
3 spring onions, sliced
2 red chillies, deseeded and thinly sliced
1 x 326g tin of sweetcorn in water, drained
4 baby courgettes, halved lengthways
115g frozen petits pois, defrosted
6 cherry tomatoes, halved
1 tablespoon reduced-salt soy sauce
1 tablespoon light miso paste
juice of 1 lime
2 teaspoons chopped coriander

Heat the oil in a frying pan, then add the onions, chillies, sweetcorn, courgettes and peas, and cook for 2 minutes, stirring regularly. Add the tomatoes, soy sauce and miso and stir until the miso combines with the other ingredients. Fold in the lime juice and coriander, and check the seasoning.

Serve at room temperature as a salad or hot as a vegetable.

Peperonata

Per serving

113 cals   3.9g fibre

3.5g fat   0.5g salt

0.5g saturates

12.9g sugar   **1.1g fat per 100g**

This is a lovely, vibrant summery dish which can be served as a salad, side order or as part of an antipasti buffet. Peppers are a good source of beta-carotene, which helps to keep the carcinogenic free radicals at bay. This is really delicious folded into scrambled eggs.

Serves 4

2 red peppers, grilled, skinned and
     deseeded, then cut in thin strips

1 yellow pepper, grilled, skinned and
     deseeded, then cut in thin strips

1 green pepper, grilled, skinned and
     deseeded, then cut in thin strips

1 tablespoon olive oil

1 red onion, thinly sliced

1 sprig thyme, leaves stripped

2 bay leaves

4 garlic cloves, crushed to a paste with
     a little salt

90ml dry white wine

1 x 400g tin chopped tomatoes

8 basil leaves ripped

salt and ground black pepper

Combine all the peppers with any cooking juices. In a frying pan heat the olive oil then add the onion and cook gently for 10–12 minutes to soften without colour.

Add the thyme, bay and garlic and cook for 3 minutes before increasing the temperature and adding the wine. Boil fast until almost all the liquid has evaporated. Add the cooked peppers and the tomato and reduce the temperature, cook gently for 20–35 minutes stirring from time to time until thick and all the flavours have melded together. Stir in the basil and season to taste.

Tip

From time to time I like to intensify the flavours by adding some chilli flakes and chopped anchovy.

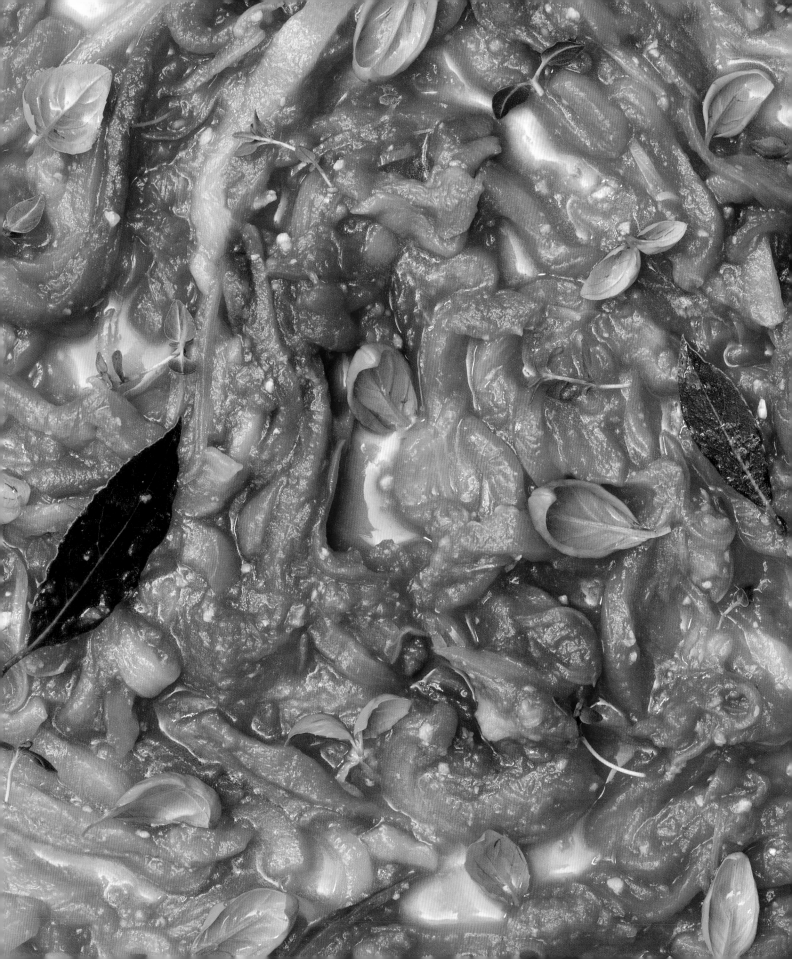

Indian roast potatoes

Per serving

266 cals   4.2g fibre
2.7g fat   0.1g salt
0.5g saturates
9.5g sugar   **0.7g fat per 100g**

So many interesting potato dishes involve the use of fat, whether it's butter, oil or dripping. What I've tried to do here is provide a potato low-fat dish that can partner your meat or fish.

Serves 4

20 new potatoes, unpeeled, each cut
    into 4 wedges
2 teaspoons vegetable oil
4 large red chillies, each cut into four
    (lengthways)
8 garlic cloves, skin on, lightly crushed
2 red onions, each cut into 6 wedges
1 teaspoon ground cumin
½ teaspoon ground coriander
½ teaspoon ground turmeric
¼ teaspoon ground chilli
½ teaspoon garam masala
1 teaspoon caster sugar
juice of 1 lime
handful of coriander leaves

Preheat the oven to 190°C/gas mark 5.

Place the potatoes in a bowl and toss with the vegetable oil. Add the remaining ingredients except the lime juice and coriander leaves, and toss really thoroughly to ensure that all the vegetables are well covered with spices.

Tip into an oven tray and roast in the oven for 45–50 minutes, shuffling the vegetables around every few minutes to make sure none are burning.

When the potatoes are cooked, remove from the oven and add the lime juice and coriander leaves, tossing until the leaves wilt.

Stock-soused spuds

Per serving

175 cals   3.8g fibre
1g fat   1.5g salt
0.2g saturates
8g sugar   **0.3g fat per 100g**

I used to be such a fan of dauphinoise potatoes, but that cream – delicious as it was – did none of us any favours. Here, I'm getting brilliant flavour but it's goodbye to all that fat.

Serves 6

1kg floury potatoes, washed, skin on,
    very thinly sliced
2 large onions, thinly sliced
8 garlic cloves, peeled and thinly sliced
1 teaspoon chopped thyme leaves
6 bay leaves
spray of olive oil
1 orange, unpeeled, thinly sliced
lots of black pepper
600ml good vegetable or chicken stock

Preheat the oven to 190°C/gas 5.

Combine the potato slices, onions, garlic, thyme and bay leaves in a bowl. Spray with oil, season and toss to combine.

Arrange half the potatoes in a lightly oiled roasting tray, pushing them flat, then make a layer of orange slices on top, followed by the remaining potato mixture; try to make the top layer into a respectable arrangement.

Pour in the stock – it will probably come up to over half the depth of the potatoes. Spray the top layer with a little oil, then cover the tray with foil.

Place in the oven for 30 minutes, then remove the foil and return to the oven to continue cooking and to brown the surface. This will take another 40 minutes.

Bacon beans with sage, rosemary and fennel

Per serving
179 cals   6.9g fibre
4g fat   1g salt
1g saturates
7g sugar   **1.4g fat per 100g**

Once you've tasted these beans, you may well forgo the weekly helping of baked beans in tomato sauce. Beans provide you with all sorts of health benefits – they are a source of protein, carbohydrate, iron and other minerals, and of course provide you with important fibre.

Serves 4

2 teaspoons olive oil

3 rashers dry-cure back bacon, fat and rind removed, cut into lardons

1 red onion, finely sliced

½ teaspoon chopped sage

½ teaspoon fennel seeds

½ sprig of rosemary, leaves stripped and finely chopped

1 mild long red chilli, deseeded and finely diced

2 x 400g tin white beans (cannellini, soisson or haricot), drained and rinsed

1 x 400g tin chopped tomatoes

1 teaspoon caster sugar

2 tablespoons chopped parsley

Heat the olive oil in a large saucepan, then add the bacon pieces and cook until golden. Add the red onion, sage, fennel seeds, rosemary and chilli to the pan, and cook over a medium heat for 8–10 minutes without colouring the onion too much.

Add the beans and tomatoes and cook gently until the sauce is thick, about 12–15 minutes, then fold in the sugar and parsley. Season to taste.

Tip

The beans taste great served on wholemeal toast or as a partner to grilled meat or fish. Vegetarians can, of course, enjoy them without the bacon.

Asian greens in black bean sauce

Per serving
91 cals   3.8g fibre
3.6g fat   1.5g salt
0.6g saturates
5.6g sugar   **1.3g fat per 100g**

I can't get enough of Chinese greens. I haven't persuaded my children to get so excited about them, though they're slowly coming round. This is a great way to eat them, the perfect accompaniment for a plain piece of meat or fish.

Serves 4

2 teaspoons sesame oil

115g sugar snap peas, topped and tailed

250g Chinese broccoli

8 baby courgettes cut in half lengthways

2 heads of pak choi cut in half lengthways

1 teaspoon garlic paste

½ teaspoon ginger paste

1 medium-hot red chilli, deseeded and chopped

90ml vegetable stock

2 tablespoons shop-bought black bean sauce

1 tablespoon kecap manis

1 teaspoon sesame seeds

Heat the oil in a wok then add the sugar snaps, broccoli, courgettes and pak choi, and stir-fry for 2 minutes. Add the garlic and ginger pastes and the chilli and stir to combine.

Pour in the stock, black bean sauce and kecap manis and cook for 1 minute.

Transfer to a warm dish and serve sprinkled with sesame seeds.

Tip

Unless you've got a Chinese supermarket in your area, some of the greens may not be available, but you can always improvise with Western greens.

French beans with cherry tomatoes

Per serving (based on 4 servings)

60 cals	2.8g fibre
2.2g fat	0.3g salt
0.3g saturates	
5.8g sugar	**1.1g fat per 100g**

It's great to eat your vegetables, but it's even better to jazz them up with a little extra flavour, especially if they're accompanying a piece of steamed fish or grilled meat. You don't have to use beans, you can try any green vegetable.

Serves 4–6

325g extra fine green beans, topped and tailed

2 teaspoons olive oil

½ onion, finely chopped

2 garlic cloves, finely sliced

2 anchovy fillets in oil, drained and patted dry with kitchen paper

1 hot red chilli, left whole

1 x 400g tin cherry tomatoes

8 basil leaves, ripped

Bring a pan of salted water to the boil and cook the beans for 3–4 minutes, leaving a little bite. Drain.

Meanwhile, heat the olive oil in a frying pan and cook the onion over a medium heat for 8 minutes. Add the garlic, anchovies and chilli and cook for 3–4 minutes more, until the anchovies start to break down.

Add the tomatoes and bring to the boil, season, then add the beans and basil. Warm through, season and serve.

Per serving (based on 6 servings)

110 cals	3.2g fibre
2.2g fat	0.3g salt
0.4g saturates	
7.6g sugar	**0.7g fat per 100g**

Fattoush with tomato dressing

This Middle Eastern salad is a mixture of fresh vibrant colour and the crunch of raw vegetables and baked pitta. I've replaced much of the olive oil with puréed tomatoes.

Serves 4–6

7 ripe tomatoes, roughly chopped

2 garlic cloves, roughly chopped

juice of 2 lemons

2 teaspoons extra virgin olive oil

2 handfuls of rocket leaves

1 tablespoon sumac

2 pitta breads

1 cucumber, peeled, cut in half lengthways, deseeded and chopped

1 red onion, thinly sliced

4 spring onions, thinly sliced at an angle

6 radishes, each cut into 6 wedges

handful of parsley leaves

12 mint leaves, shredded

2 Baby Gem lettuces, leaves separated

Preheat the oven to 180°C/gas mark 4.

In a food-processor, blend half the tomatoes with the garlic, lemon juice, olive oil, half the rocket leaves and the sumac until smooth. Season with salt and pepper and set aside.

Split the pitta bread in half then break into irregular pieces. Place on a rack in the oven and cook for about 15 minutes, until crisp and brittle, then remove and set aside to cool.

In a bowl, combine the remaining tomatoes, cucumber, red onion, spring onions, radishes, parsley, mint and lettuce.

Just before serving, dress the salad with the tomato vinaigrette and scatter with the crisp pitta pieces.

Asian pork and lychee salad

Per serving

155 cals   2.2g fibre

3g fat   0.9g salt

0.1g saturates

16.9g sugar   **1.3g fat per 100g**

Ever since I was a boy I have loved tinned lychees even more than the fresh ones, which appear to be picked before the sugars have developed. Pork is one of our lowest-fat meats and I tend to cook it with a hint of mint to retain its juiciness. It's your call, but I can tell you that pork is safe to eat even when a little pink.

Serves 4

spray of vegetable oil

250g pork fillets or tenderloin, any visible fat removed

12 tinned lychees, drained

½ red pepper, deseeded and cut into thin strips

½ yellow pepper, deseeded and cut into thin strips

1 Asian pear, cored and cut into batons or thin crescents, seeds removed

zest of 2 limes

2cm piece of root ginger, peeled and cut into julienne (thin batons)

55g watercress, large stems discarded

12 mint leaves, shredded

6 basil leaves, shredded

4 spring onions, thinly sliced on the diagonal

25g beansprouts, soaked in iced water

1 tablespoon pink pickled ginger, drained and cut into thin strips

DRESSING:

lime juice from the 2 limes (above)

1 teaspoon finely chopped garlic

1 bird's eye chilli, very thinly shredded

1 tablespoon pickled ginger juice

1 tablespoon rice vinegar

1 tablespoon nam pla (fish sauce)

2 teaspoons liquid honey

Spray a non-stick frying pan with oil and place over a medium heat. Add the pork, brown all over and cook until done to your liking, about 10 minutes. Remove and allow to cool enough to handle.

Combine all the ingredients for the dressing, stirring to combine.

Slice the pork thinly and add to the dressing, tossing to combine. Allow to stand for 15 minutes.

Toss together all the remaining salad ingredients, so everything is evenly distributed, then add the pork slices and dressing. Toss again, then serve immediately.

Tip

This recipe works equally well with cooked chicken breast. If you can't find Asian pears just use conference.

Crab and grapefruit salad

Per serving

154 cals   2g fibre
5.2g fat   3g salt
0.7g saturates
7.9g sugar   **1.8g fat per 100g**

There's nothing nicer than fresh crab. However, if you're like me, you don't enjoy picking out the flesh from the shell. In good fishmongers, you can usually find freshly picked crabmeat, which has often been pasteurised first but tastes good. If not, *avoid* the frozen kind and go instead for tinned crab in brine, which is pretty good.

Serves 4–6

¼ Napa or Chinese cabbage (150g), very thinly shredded

½ cucumber, deseeded and cut into 1cm dice

2 ripe tomatoes, deseeded and diced

12 mint leaves, shredded

1 ruby grapefruit, skinned, pith removed and segments cut from between the membranes

4 spring onions, thinly sliced on the diagonal

350g fresh or tinned crabmeat, drained and picked over for rogue pieces of shell

DRESSING:

juice from membranes of the grapefruit

1 garlic clove, crushed to a paste with a little salt

2 teaspoons sweet chilli sauce

1 teaspoon grated root ginger

2 tablespoons nam pla (fish sauce)

1 teaspoon caster sugar

2 bird's eye chillies, finely chopped

For the dressing, simply place all the ingredients in a clean jam jar, put the lid on and shake.

Combine all the salad ingredients and add enough dressing to coat. Toss well and serve.

Tip

When segmenting a grapefruit, cut between the membranes holding the peeled grapefruit over a bowl to catch any juices, then squeeze out any juices from the core and the membranes.

A different green salad

Per serving
108 cals   4.1g fibre
4.7g fat   1.1g salt
0.7g saturates
4g sugar   **3g fat per 100g**

This chunky legume salad with the vibrant colours of spring greens is designed for texture, taste and health.

Serves 4

1 teaspoon grated ginger

2 garlic cloves, crushed to a paste
   with a little salt

1 red chilli, finely sliced

2 teaspoons vegetable or peanut oil

1 teaspoon mustard seeds

4 spring onions, thinly sliced on
   the diagonal

juice of 2 lemons

1 tablespoon nam pla (fish sauce)

1 teaspoon caster sugar

115g extra fine French beans, topped
   and tailed and cut into 2cm pieces

200g frozen petits pois, defrosted

175g frozen, podded edamame beans,
   defrosted

12 mint leaves, shredded

½ bunch of coriander, roughly chopped

Place the ginger, garlic and chilli in a pan with the oil and gently heat to release flavour rather than cook. Increase the heat, add the mustard seeds and cook until they're jumping. Turn off the heat then add the spring onions, lemon juice, nam pla and sugar. Toss to combine, season, then set aside.

Meanwhile, heat a deep pan of salted water to boiling then add the French beans and cook for 2 minutes. Add the peas and edamame beans and cook for a further minute.

Drain the vegetables and add to the Asian dressing in the other pan. Add the herbs and toss to combine. Serve cold, hot or at room temperature.

Tip

Edamame beans, which are a soy bean and a good source of protein, are becoming more widely available, but if you can't find them substitute with frozen baby broad beans.

Cool and hot cucumber salad

Per serving
22 cals   0.9g fibre
0.2g fat   1.3g salt
0g saturates
3.4g sugar   **0.1g fat per 100g**

This salad makes a great accompaniment for grilled fish, such as salmon. It has a wonderful fresh taste.

Serves 4

1 large cucumber, thinly sliced

1 teaspoon salt

2 medium-heat, long green chillies,
   deseeded and finely diced

1 red chilli, deseeded and finely diced

1 tablespoon chopped coriander

1 teaspoon chopped mint

2 tablespoons cider vinegar

½ teaspoon Tabasco sauce

1 teaspoon caster sugar

Place the cucumber slices in a colander and sprinkle with the salt and toss well. Place over a bowl or in the sink and allow the salt to extract the cucumber water for 20 minutes; then rinse under running water and pat dry.

Combine the remaining ingredients in a bowl, add the cucumber and check the seasoning. Allow the flavours to develop for 20 minutes before serving.

Tip

If you want to keep the cucumber bright green, add the vinegar only just before serving.

Low-fat jewelled couscous

Per serving
420 cals
2.2g fat
0.4g saturates
22.2g sugar

3.1g fibre
0.9g salt

0.8g fat per 100g

Couscous is very bland in its natural state but with my addition you've got yourself a great salad or accompaniment to a tagine or stew.

Serves 6

300ml chicken stock
300ml water
500g couscous
grated zest of 1 lemon
2 teaspoons extra virgin olive oil
55g dried cherries
55g frozen petits pois, defrosted
115g ready-to-eat apricots, chopped
55g sultanas
1 courgette, coarsely grated
2 heaped tablespoons chopped
   flat-leaf parsley
2 heaped tablespoons chopped coriander

Heat the stock and water in a pan until boiling. Pour in the couscous in a thin, steady stream then stir in the lemon zest. Cover with clingfilm and set aside for 5 minutes to allow the grains to swell. Fluff up the grains with a fork so that they separate. (You can prepare ahead to this stage.)

Return the couscous to the heat and drizzle over the olive oil. Cook gently for a few minutes, stirring with the fork to fluff up the grains, then remove from the heat. Fold in the remaining ingredients and season to taste. If not serving immediately, tip the couscous into an ovenproof dish, cover with foil and keep warm in the bottom of a moderate oven until you're ready to serve.

Roast carrot and beetroot salad with cottage cheese

Per serving
131 cals
3.8g fat
0.8g saturates
15.7g sugar

3.8g fibre
0.5g salt

1.5g fat per 100g

Roasting the carrot and beetroot caramelises the edges and intensifies the sweetness of the vegetables. The choice of salad leaves must be yours, but I enjoy a bag of wild rocket and watercress.

Serves 4

16 baby beetroots, washed
1 tablespoon olive oil
2 bay leaves
6 sprigs of thyme
12 baby carrots, scrubbed but left whole
8 garlic cloves, unpeeled
3 tablespoons sherry vinegar
2 teaspoons runny honey
1 bag of mixed salad leaves
115g low-fat cottage cheese

Preheat the oven to 200°C/gas mark 6.

Toss the beetroot in the olive oil with the bay leaves and thyme. Place in a roasting tray, season and roast for 45 minutes. Add the carrots and garlic then return to the oven and cook for a further 35 minutes.

Remove the beetroot and garlic and, when cool enough to handle, squeeze them out of their skins. Return to the roasting pan and toss all the vegetables with the vinegar and honey.

Arrange the salad leaves on four plates and scatter over the vegetables and garlic with their juices. Crumble over the cottage cheese and serve.

Tip

If you can't find raw baby beetroots, buy cooked beetroots and add with the carrots or cut larger beetroots into small wedges and follow the recipe above.

Winter vegetables in a pot

Per serving
196 cals   7.7g fibre
4.9g fat   0.2g salt
0.8g saturates
15.2g sugar   **1.5g fat per 100g**

Forget the protein, I could eat a pot of these vegetables just as they are. I've chosen my favourite vegetables, but you can vary the mixture depending on your likes and dislikes.

Serves 4

2 onions, cut into 8 wedges

2 parsnips, peeled and quartered

12 Brussels sprouts, trimmed

8 Chantenay carrots, topped and tailed

2 sticks of celery, each cut crossways into 3

½ butternut squash, deseeded, skin removed and cut into manageable chunks

1 tablespoon chopped thyme

8 unpeeled garlic cloves

175ml dry martini or dry white wine

2 tablespoons extra virgin olive oil

1 x 400g tin cannellini beans, drained and rinsed

175ml water

TO SERVE:

1 teaspoon finely chopped garlic

grated zest of 1 unwaxed lemon

3 tablespoons chopped parsley

2 tablespoons sherry vinegar

2 teaspoons runny honey

Put everything except the beans and serving ingredients in an ovenproof, lidded pot and toss with the oil and some salt and pepper. Allow to sit for 30 minutes to allow the flavours to develop.

Preheat the oven to 220°C/gas mark 7.

Cover the pot with a lid, place in the centre of the oven and cook the vegetables for 1 hour. After this time, fold in the cannellini beans along with the water then return to the oven, uncovered, and cook for another 20 minutes.

Combine the serving ingredients and, just before you're ready to eat, stir into the vegetables and check the seasoning.

Summer peas with bacon, lettuce and mint

Per serving
115 cals   4.5g fibre
5.5g fat   1.6g salt
1.3g saturates
5.1g sugar   **2.4g fat per 100g**

This side dish is based on '*petits pois à la française*', a fab combination of flavours. Unless you grow your own, I would always recommend using frozen petits pois because they usually have more vitamins than so-called 'fresh', which may have been hanging around for a few days since being picked.

Serves 4

1 tablespoon olive oil

4 spring onions, finely sliced

3 rashers of dry-cure back bacon, fat and
    rind removed, cut into lardons

1 garlic clove, crushed to a paste with
    a little salt

2 Baby Gem lettuces, washed
    and shredded

325g frozen petits pois, defrosted

150ml vegetable stock

1 teaspoon caster sugar

2 teaspoons chopped mint

In a medium saucepan, heat the oil with the spring onions and bacon and cook gently for 4–6 minutes. Add the garlic and lettuce and cook, stirring regularly, for 5 minutes until the lettuce wilts.

Add the peas, stock and sugar, increase the heat and boil vigorously for 5 minutes. Fold in the mint and season; it shouldn't need much salt but a few twists of pepper will add a nice dimension.

Curried peas with mint and tomato

Per serving
67 cals   4.4g fibre
3.6g fat   0.2g salt
0.5g saturates
4.7g sugar   **1.8g fat per 100g**

Peas are loved by almost everybody, but they can become repetitive so here's a recipe to ring the changes.

Serves 4

2 teaspoons vegetable oil

2 teaspoons brown mustard seeds

1 teaspoon grated ginger

4 spring onions, finely sliced

1 red chilli, deseeded and finely diced

1 teaspoon ground cumin

½ teaspoon ground coriander

¼ teaspoon ground fennel

½ teaspoon ground turmeric

3 tomatoes, roughly chopped

150ml water

½ teaspoon garam masala

1 tablespoon chopped mint

1 teaspoon chopped coriander

325g frozen petits pois, defrosted

Heat the oil in a saucepan. Add the mustard seeds, wait until they start to pop, then add the ginger, spring onions, chilli and ground spices. Cook for a minute then add the tomatoes and water.

Bring everything to the boil, cook for 3 minutes, then add the garam masala, mint, coriander and peas and cook for 6 minutes. Check the seasoning and serve.

Smoked chicken and parsley salad

Per serving

283 cals   4.3g fibre

7g fat   1.7g salt

1.2g saturates

3.9g sugar   **2g fat per 100g**

The smokiness of the chicken breast contrasts nicely with the mild new potatoes, while the flat-leaf parsley leaves combined with the rocket and watercress add another dimension to the dish. And then there's that lovely hot/cold sensation.

Serves 4

450g Pink Fir or Charlotte potatoes, each cut lengthways into 6 wedges

225g frozen edamame beans, defrosted

115g extra fine French beans

225g smoked chicken breasts, skinned and thinly sliced

4 spring onions, thinly sliced

55g rocket leaves

1 bunch of flat-leaf parsley, leave picked, stalks retained

55g watercress, tough stems removed

HERB DRESSING:

parsley stalks from above, roughly chopped

1 tablespoon olive oil

4 tablespoons 0% fat Greek yogurt

2 teaspoons Dijon mustard

1 sprig of tarragon, leaves only, finely chopped

1 tablespoon Lilliput (baby) capers, drained

4 cornichons, finely chopped

Heat a pan of salted water and cook the potatoes until tender, about 15 minutes. Add the edamame and French beans and cook for a further 4 minutes.

Meanwhile, make the dressing in a food-processor: blend together the parsley stalks, olive oil and yogurt with a little salt and pepper until smooth. Pass through a fine sieve into a bowl and fold in the remaining ingredients. Mix well and check the seasoning.

When the potatoes and beans have cooked, drain and set aside. Combine the chicken breast with the spring onions, rocket, parsley and watercress. Fold in the warm vegetables then add enough of the dressing to coat. Serve immediately.

Tip

The bulk of the salad can be made ahead, as can the dressing, but don't cook or add the vegetables until just before serving.

A potato salad with bite

Per serving

243 cals	4.2g fibre
1.1g fat	1.4g salt
0.1g saturates	
8.2g sugar	**0.3g fat per 100g**

With all my potato salads, I like to dress them warm so that the potatoes absorb the flavours, and I also like to slightly overcook old floury potatoes so that their edges are starting to break up.

Serves 4

1kg floury potatoes, peeled and cut into 2.5cm dice

1 onion, finely chopped

2 tablespoons Lilliput (baby) capers, drained

4 anchovy fillets, drained and chopped

6 cornichons (baby gherkins), thinly sliced

2 sweet gherkins, cut into 5mm dice

4 tablespoons chopped parsley

2 tablespoons snipped chives

2 teaspoons chopped mint

½ teaspoon ground white pepper

5 tablespoons 0% fat yogurt

Cook the potatoes in salted water until tender, about 15–20 minutes. Drain well in the colander, tossing them around so that the edges break up a little.

Meanwhile, as the potatoes are cooking, combine the onion, capers, anchovies, cornichons, gherkins, herbs and pepper in a bowl. Fold in the yogurt and season.

While the potatoes are still warm, add the herb dressing and stir to combine. Serve the salad at room temperature.

Tip

For a better GI rating you could use new potatoes, but the texture won't be the same.

Per serving

139 cals	2.4g fibre
5g fat	0.9g salt
2.9g saturates	
15g sugar	**2.4g fat per 100g**

An autumn orchard salad

This is a great autumn salad when British orchard fruits are at their best.

Serves 4

55g Roquefort cheese, crumbled

200ml 0% fat Greek yogurt

1 tablespoon snipped chives

½ teaspoon chopped tarragon

4 cornichons, thinly sliced

1 teaspoon baby capers, drained

1 teaspoon lemon juice

1 teaspoon runny honey

1 Conference pear, halved, cored, then thinly sliced

2 Cox's apples, halved, cored, then thinly sliced

1 bag washed watercress and rocket

Combine the Roquefort and yogurt and mash well to combine. Add the herbs, cornichons, capers, lemon juice and honey and season to taste.

Fold the fruit into the dressing and toss to combine.

Arrange the salad leaves on four plates then scatter over the fruit mixture, arranging neatly if preferred.

Tip

You could throw in a few blackberries for added orchard flavours, in which case change the tarragon to mint.

Roast cauliflower with beans and pak choi

Per serving

78 cals   3.8g fibre

1.6g fat   0.9g salt

0.3g saturates

8.3g sugar   **0.6g fat per 100g**

Boiled cauliflower doesn't do it for me – it cries out for cheese sauce, but as we all know that's not allowed to feature in our low-fat diet. Recently, however, I had roast cauliflower and was impressed; it adds a lovely nuttiness to the flavour and the cauliflower retains a little crunch.

Serves 6

1 cauliflower (approx. 700g), cut into bite-sized florets, the central core discarded

1 onion, cut into 8 wedges

3 garlic cloves, crushed to a paste with a little salt

spray of vegetable oil

4 spring onions, finely sliced on the diagonal

2 medium-heat chillies, finely sliced

60ml water or vegetable stock

175g extra fine French beans, topped, tailed and cut into 2.5cm pieces

2 heads of pak choi, cut in quarters lengthways

1 tablespoon chopped coriander roots and stems (see Tip)

1 tablespoon reduced-salt soy sauce

1 tablespoon oyster sauce

2 teaspoons runny honey

1 tablespoon coriander leaves

Preheat the oven to 200°C/gas mark 6.

Place the cauliflower in a bowl with the onion, garlic and spray all over with the oil. Season with salt and ground black pepper then place in a roasting tray in the oven and cook for 20 minutes, turning regularly. Remove and set aside.

Six minutes before the end of the roasting time, spray a wok with oil and, over a high heat, stir-fry the spring onions and chilli for 1 minute. Add the water and bring to the boil, then add the beans and cook for 3 minutes. Add the pak choi and cook for a further 1 minute.

Add the coriander roots and stems, soy and oyster sauces and honey and stir-fry for 1 minute. Finally, add the hot cauliflower mixture and toss to combine. Sprinkle with coriander leaves.

Tip

The Thais use coriander roots and stems a lot in their cooking, but you might find it hard to find bunches with roots unless you use an Asian supermarket. Alternatively, just use finely chopped stems.

Purple sprouting broccoli with cannellini beans and spinach

I'm not going to tell you how to cook your vegetables, but I will suggest how to jazz them up to make that plain bit of chicken or fish a little more exciting. If you like anchovies, you'll love this, and it would go perfectly with some roast cod.

Serves 4

1 red onion, cut into 8 wedges

spray of olive oil

4 garlic cloves, crushed to a paste with a little salt

4 anchovy fillets, roughly chopped

pinch of dried oregano

pinch of chilli flakes

2 x 400g tin cannellini beans, rinsed and drained

400g purple sprouting broccoli, woody stems removed

2 handfuls of baby spinach leaves, wet from washing

Put a deep pan of salted water on to boil.

Meanwhile, place the onion wedges in a non-stick saucepan, spray with oil and cook over a gentle heat for 12–15 minutes, to soften but not colour. Add the garlic, anchovies, oregano and chilli and toss to combine. Cook for 2 minutes until the anchovies break down. Add the beans to the onions, toss to combine, and season well.

While the onions are cooking, put the broccoli in the boiling water and cook for 6–8 minutes. I want the broccoli to be a bit softer than you would normally cook it and absorb some water. Then, using a slotted spoon, scoop the broccoli from the pan, allowing some water to cling to it. Spoon into the beans and combine quite vigorously so that the broccoli heads break up leaving the beans speckled with green.

Finally, fold in the spinach and cook until wilted, about 2 minutes.

A Piedmontese-style pepper

Per serving

139 cals
6.5g fat
3.8g saturates
12.4g sugar

3.5g fibre
0.6g salt

2.4g fat per 100g

This is a very popular starter at my pub, The Greyhound. We put it on the menu whenever my greengrocer sends peppers by the box at an attractive price! And it is delicious topped with a slice of low-fat mozzarella.

Serves 4

4 tomatoes, cored

4 red or yellow peppers, halved lengthways through the stalk, deseeded

3 garlic cloves, thinly sliced

16 basil leaves

4 anchovy fillets, each cut in 4

spray of olive oil

100g mozzarella cheese, cut into 8 slices

Place the tomatoes in a bowl and pour over boiling water, leave for 1 minute, then plunge into cold water. Remove the skins, then halve the tomatoes.

Preheat the oven to 200°C/gas mark 6.

In the bottom of each pepper, place a few slices of garlic, a couple of basil leaves and a couple of pieces of anchovy. Leave for 10 minutes.

Push half a tomato into each pepper cavity, squashing it in tightly so that it tucks in under the edge of the pepper and spray lightly with olive oil. Place in a roasting tray, ideally on a rack, and place in the oven. Cook for 20 minutes then turn the oven down to 180°C/gas mark 4 and cook for a further 25 minutes. For the last 8–12 minutes of cooking, top each pepper with a slice of mozzarella and cook until melted.

Spiced cauliflower with red lentil sauce

Per serving

269 cals
6.1g fat
0.9g saturates
9.4g sugar

6g fibre
1.5g salt

1.5g fat per 100g

This is a really 'meaty' vegetarian dish that has lots of flavour and the crunch of undercooked cauliflower.

Serves 4

1 tablespoon vegetable oil

1 onion, finely chopped

3 garlic cloves, crushed to a paste with a little salt

2 tablespoons ground cumin

2 teaspoons ground coriander

200g red lentils, rinsed

300ml vegetable stock

1 x 400g tin cherry tomatoes

1 small cauliflower, broken into small florets

spray of vegetable oil

2 teaspoons chopped coriander

In a large saucepan, heat the vegetable oil and cook the onion and garlic gently for 8–10 minutes. Add half the spices and the lentils and stir to combine.

Add the stock and cherry tomatoes, bring to the boil, then reduce the heat and simmer until the lentils start to break down, about 25 minutes.

Meanwhile, spray the cauliflower florets with vegetable oil then dust with the remaining spices. Cook in a frying pan over a high heat to brown the cauliflower all over, add to the lentils and cook for 2 minutes.

Garnish with coriander and serve with rice.

Puddings and cakes

Campari and orange sorbet

Per serving	
170 cals	0.1g fibre
0g fat	0g salt
0g saturates	
40.6g sugar	**0g fat per 100g**

A great palate cleanser that is perfect to finish a meal, light and cooling and you're also getting loads of vitamin C plus a smattering of potassium and carotene which will help you fight off the winter chills.

Serves 4

juice of 6 and the grated rind
  of 1 orange
115g caster sugar
2 sprigs mint
3 tablespoons Campari

Heat the orange juice with the rind, sugar and mint in a non-reactive saucepan until boiling and the sugar has dissolved. Allow to cool to room temperature, add the Campari and remove the mint and discard. Pour into your ice cream machine and follow the manufacturer's instructions. Keep in the freezer.

This is best eaten on the day it is made as home-made sorbets tend to go hard. If this happens, allow the sorbet to defrost then re-churn.

Tip

If you don't have an ice-cream machine you'd be better turning this recipe into a granita, which is a water ice. Simply tip the cooled mixture into a shallow tray and place in the freezer. After about 1 hour when the mix is starting to freeze, break it up with a whisk and repeat every 15 minutes until you have a frozen slush.

Affogato – adult coffee and ice cream

Per serving	
111 cals	0g fibre
3.1g fat	0.1g salt
1.8g saturates	
14.7g sugar	**2.4g fat per 100g**

I rarely eat puddings but I do love an after-dinner coffee. This simple pud is an Italian classic that demands fresh coffee, which happens to be a good source of riboflavin, one of the B vitamins. Like most of your diet, coffee should be taken in sensible moderation.

Serves 4

4 scoops reduced-fat vanilla ice cream
4 freshly made double espressos
8 teaspoons Tia Maria or coffee liqueur

Place 1 scoop of ice cream 4 cappuccino cups or glass bowls.
Pour over the espresso, sweetened if required, then top off with Tia Maria. Serve *immediately*.

Tip

You can mix and match the liqueur using brandy or whisky for instance instead of Tia Maria.

Zabaglione-glazed raspberries

Per serving

117 cals   2.8g fibre

3.7g fat   0g salt

1.1g saturates

16.8g sugar   **2.5g fat per 100g**

Zabaglione is a classic Italian recipe in its own right, of course, but it also makes a great topping for soft fruits. Here I'm using raspberries, but feel free to ring the changes. This recipe is the original 'foam', conceived long before the penchant for foams became commonplace among modern young chefs.

Serves 4

450g fresh raspberries

2 egg yolks

2 tablespoons caster sugar

2 tablespoons sweet sherry or Marsala

2 tablespoons orange juice

Arrange the raspberries in four shallow heatproof gratin dishes.

Combine the remaining ingredients in a bowl and set it over a saucepan of simmering water, making sure that the water doesn't touch the bottom of the bowl. With an electric whisk (or by hand if you're fit), whisk the mixture for 8–10 minutes or until it's light, frothy and holds its own shape. You will find that you want to stop after 2–3 minutes but don't because the eggs won't have 'cooked' and the foam will collapse very quickly.

Preheat the grill.

Spoon the foam over the raspberries then grill until browned in patches. Beware, the colour can change in an instant and you could end up with delicious scrambled egg!

Per serving

306 cals   4.1g fibre

5.3g fat   0.1g salt

0.5g saturates

53.2g sugar   **1.8g fat per 100g**

Roast peaches with amaretti and raspberries

This recipe brings out the sweet, juicy flavour of a peach. I've left the skins on for fibre; if you want to remove, make a small cut top and bottom and blanch them in boiling water for 1 minute. Cool, then peel.

Serves 4

4 peaches, halved, stones removed

8 amaretti biscuits

3 tablespoons soft dark brown sugar

2 tablespoons amaretto liqueur (optional)

270ml 0% fat Greek yogurt

2 tablespoons sifted icing sugar

225g raspberries

Preheat the oven to 190°C/gas mark 5.

Place the peaches cut-side up in a baking tray. Smash the amaretti biscuits in a bag with a rolling pin. You're not looking for a powder, just small chunks. Combine the biscuits with the brown sugar, and liqueur if using.

Fill the peach cavity with the biscuit mixture then place in the oven and cook for 25 minutes, or until the peach has softened and caramelised. Keep an eye out for burning, if so reduce the oven temperature.

Meanwhile, place the yogurt in a bowl with the icing sugar and raspberries then whisk vigorously to break up the fruits, creating a pink chunky sauce.

Serve the cold sauce with the hot peaches.

Raspberry pancakes with blueberry sauce

Per serving
373 cals   3.3g fibre
4.8g fat   0.7g salt
1.2g saturates
40.6g sugar   **1.7g fat per 100g**

These American-style pancakes are also great for lazy weekend breakfasts but they make a delicious dessert and are especially loved by children.

Serves 6

1 large Bramley apple, peeled, quartered and cored, then roughly diced
3 tablespoons water
2 tablespoons lemon juice
4 tablespoons caster sugar
1 free-range egg, separated
2 egg yolks
550g 0% fat yogurt
275g self-raising flour
225g raspberries, mashed with a fork
spray of vegetable oil

SAUCE:

175g blueberries, roughly chopped
4 tablespoons blackcurrant jam
1 tablespoon caster sugar
1 tablespoon lime juice

Place the apple in a saucepan with the water, lemon juice and half the sugar and cook over a gentle heat until the apple breaks down to a purée, about 12–15 minutes. Allow to cool.

Beat the three egg whites to soft peaks then add the remaining sugar and beat until glossy and forms stiff peaks.

Beat together the egg yolk, apple purée, yogurt, flour and crushed raspberries, then fold in one spoonful of beaten egg white to slacken the mixture before folding in the remaining egg whites.

Heat a large, non-stick frying pan and spray with oil. Drop tablespoons of raspberry batter onto the frying pan and cook for about 2 minutes until little bubbles appear on the surface. Flip over and cook for another minute. Keep warm in a low oven. Cook until all the batter is used.

Meanwhile, make the sauce by placing all the ingredients in a saucepan and cooking for 3–4 minutes, stirring constantly. Serve it warm or hot, chunky or smooth. I like a chunky sauce, but feel free to blend it in a food-processor.

Serve the pancakes with the blueberry sauce.

Tip

You can serve extra raspberries for a more substantial pudding.

Red fruits with Pedro Ximénez sherry

This is a fast, standby pud that is really easy as long as you have the sherry. PX is a really chocolatey sherry, the flavour of which is unique; you'll have to search it out through the internet or a good off-licence, but if you can't find it a normal cream or sweet sherry will do, though it will be second best. On the health front, weight for weight, strawberries contain more vitamin C than citrus fruit.

Serves 4

225g strawberries, hulled and halved

225g raspberries

85g redcurrants, picked off the stalks (optional)

2 tablespoons Pedro Ximénez sherry

1 teaspoon chopped mint

2 teaspoons caster sugar

4 tablespoons 0% fat Greek yogurt

2 teaspoons lime juice

2 teaspoons runny honey

Combine the fruits with the sherry, mint and sugar, and leave to macerate for 30 minutes.

Meanwhile, combine the yogurt with the lime juice and honey.

When ready to serve, share the fruits between four glass bowls or tumblers and top with a dollop of yogurt.

Tip

You could use low-fat crème fraîche instead of the yogurt, but note that this will increase the fat content quite considerably (above 3g per 100g) so save this one for a special treat.

Summer pudding

Per serving

220 cals	5.1g fibre
1.1g fat	0.5g salt
0.3g saturates	
29.4g sugar	**0.5g fat per 100g**

This delicious summer pudding is the perfect low-fat dessert.

Serves 8

900g raspberries
225g redcurrants, picked over
50g blackcurrants, picked over
125g golden caster sugar
125ml raspberry liqueur (such as crème de framboise), optional
10–12 slices of day-old wholegrain bread, crusts removed
extra berries, to decorate

Sprinkle the fruit with the sugar and toss gently to combine. Cover and ideally leave to macerate for 2 hours.

Tip the fruit and resulting juices into a non-reactive saucepan with the liqueur and cook over a medium heat for 3–4 minutes to release some more juices.

Meanwhile, line a 1.8-litre pudding basin with clingfilm, then dip the bread into the red fruit juices and lay on the clingfilm, making sure that the slices of bread overlap slightly and cover the sides and bottom of the basin completely.

Using a slotted spoon, fill up the bread mould with fruit. Pour over half the juices, then cover the fruit completely with more bread slices. Cover with clingfilm, then top with a plate that fits inside the rim of the basin. Place a heavy weight on top of the plate and refrigerate overnight.

When you're ready to serve, turn the pudding over onto a shallow, but not flat, dish and remove the basin and clingfilm. Pour over the reserved juices and serve with a few loose berries.

Per serving (based on 8 servings)

273 cals	1g fibre
3.8g fat	0.4g salt
1.2g saturates	
46.5g sugar	**2.5g fat per 100g**

Saucy chocolate pudding

I used to eat a Betty Crocker version of this self-saucing pudding when I was a child and I found it fascinating that the sauce which started on the top ended up on the bottom...well now I know.

Serves 6–8

55g low-fat spread
120ml skimmed milk
2 teaspoons Kahlua or Tia Maria (optional)
175g caster sugar
150g self-raising flour
2 tablespoons cocoa powder
175g dark soft brown sugar
500ml boiling water

Preheat the oven to 160°C/gas mark 3. Lightly oil a baking dish that holds 1.5 litres and has sides approximately 2.5cm deep.

Melt the spread in the milk over a medium heat. Remove from the heat then whisk in the liqueur, if using, the sugar, flour and half the cocoa. Spoon the mixture into your baking dish.

Combine the sugar and remaining cocoa and sprinkle over the batter, then gently pour over the water Place in the oven and bake for 50–60 minutes until firm. Remove from the oven and let it sit for 10 minutes before serving.

Apple and orange sponge pudding

Not steamed but a similar effect, this pud is low in fat so you can enjoy it without feeling guilty. Play around with your fruit content, so many combos work; apple and pear, apple and blackberry, apple and raspberry, mango and pineapple and so on, the process remains the same.

Serves 6

2 medium Bramley apples, peeled, quartered and cored

2 Cox's Orange Pippin apples, peeled, quartered and cored

3 oranges, segmented and juice squeezed from the membrane, keep the juice and zest from 1 orange

40g caster sugar

¼ teaspoon ground cinnamon

2 tablespoons orange liqueur (optional)

2 free-range eggs

55g caster sugar

1 tablespoon cornflour, sifted

1 tablespoon plain flour, sifted

3 tablespoons self-raising flour, sifted

Preheat the oven to 180°C/gas mark 4.

Slice the apples and put in a saucepan with the juice from the oranges, the sugar and ground cinnamon. Bring to the boil, cover with a lid and cook for 12–15 minutes over a medium heat. Fold in the orange liqueur, if using.

While the apples are cooking, make the sponge by beating the eggs and sugar together, ideally with an electric whisk for about 5 minutes until pale and frothy. Fold in the sifted flours and the orange zest.

Spoon the apple and mixture into a 1½ litre baking dish and then gently spread with the sponge. Bake in the oven for 30 minutes or until the sponge is springy and golden. Serve with low-fat custard.

Toffee bananas

So simple, so popular, a crunchy toffee coating and a soft centre – perfect with some low-fat fromage frais or ice cream.

Makes 12 sticks
Serves 4

3 ripe bananas, each peeled and cut into four on the diagonal

juice of 1 lemon

250g caster sugar

8 tablespoons water

1 tablespoon sesame seeds

Toss the banana pieces in the lemon juice to prevent discolouration and to add a little tartness. Place one banana piece on the end of a skewer.

Place the sugar and water in a saucepan and warm over a medium heat. Have a bowl of water with a pastry brush to brush the sides of the pan to prevent crystals forming. Cook until the caramel has reached a pale golden colour, remove from the heat and swirl the pan gently to even the colour.

Have another bowl of cold water on standby. Dip each banana into the caramel, hold for 30 seconds then lift out, sprinkle with a few sesame seeds and plunge for 3 seconds in the cold water to set the caramel.

Serve immediately.

Apple and blackberry brûlées

Per serving

249 cals   1.9g fibre

2.2g fat   0.3g salt

0.7g saturates

51.1g sugar   **0.7g fat per 100g**

We all need to spoil ourselves with a pud from time to time but low-fat versions of full-fat favourites can often be disappointing. This is based on a crème caramel recipe, but I've slashed the fat content by making a custard using skimmed milk and just one egg yolk with extra whites (which are fat-free).

Serves 4

6 tablespoons caster sugar
  + 1 tablespoon for glazing

2 tablespoons water

2 Cox's apples, peeled, cored
  and diced

115g blackberries

1 whole egg

2 egg whites

600ml skimmed milk

nutmeg for dusting

Heat half the sugar and the 2 tablespoons of water in a saucepan until it starts to turn a golden caramel colour, occasionally swirling the pan and brushing down the sides just above the sugar line with a wet brush.

Working quickly, (the sugar will turn from golden to bitter dark very quickly) add the apple and cook, stirring regularly, for 2 minutes. Fold in the blackberries, stirring to combine.

Meanwhile, whisk the egg with the egg whites until thoroughly combined.

Bring the milk to the boil then whisk into the egg mix. Fold in the remaining sugar apart from the glazing sugar. Stir until the sugar has dissolved.

Preheat the oven to 160°C/gas mark 3.

Spoon the apple mix into the bottom of four ramekins, pour on the egg custard and remove any bubbles from the surface with a teaspoon or kitchen paper. Then dust the surface with a little nutmeg.

Stand the ramekins in a deep roasting tray and pour in enough hot water around them to come halfway up the sides.

Bake in the preheated oven for approximately 1 hour or until set. Allow to cool, then refrigerate.

Sprinkle the tops with the caster sugar for glazing and use a blow torch or hot grill to carmelise the surface until golden with hints of dark. **Do not refrigerate after glazing the surface.**

Tip

Try different fruits in the base; pear and walnut, raspberry and blueberry, pineapple and mango, papaya and passion fruit.

Something for elevenses

Per serving

208 cals	4.7g fibre
2.2g fat	0g salt
0.4g saturates	
29.1g sugar	**2.9g fat per 100g**

We're all entitled to a snack and yet so many are high in fats that often it's hard to find something suitable. I hope you'll enjoy this bar, but don't have too many as the dried fruits are high in sugar.

Makes 9

325g of your favourite dried fruits (I like dried apples, apricots, pears and blueberries)
200g 'no nuts' muesli
½ teaspoon mixed spice
½ teaspoon cinnamon
¼ teaspoon five spice powder
75ml hibiscus or pomegranate juice
2 tablespoons runny honey
65g wholemeal flour
spray of oil

Pulse the dried fruit in a food-processor until well chopped but not puréed. Combine the fruit with the muesli and spices.

Meanwhile heat the juice and honey in a large saucepan then stir in the flour followed by the muesli mixture, stir well to combine.

Preheat the oven to 200°C/gas mark 6.

Line a 25cm square or rectangular shallow baking dish with parchment paper and lightly spray with oil. Tip the mixture into the dish and smooth over the contents.

Bake in the oven for 25 minutes, checking from time to time to make sure they are not getting too brown; if they are, reduce the oven temperature to 180°C/gas mark 4.

Allow to cool, turn out, then peel back the paper and cut into squares or rectangles, depending on the shape of your tray. Store in an airtight container for up to 1 week.

Tip

I'm going through a hibiscus drink phase but feel free to use another juice such as apple.

Fruit bread biscotti

Per serving

22 cals　　　　0.1g fibre

0g fat　　　　　0g salt

0g saturates

3.4g sugar　　　**0.5g fat per 100g**

These brittle biscuits are inspired by the Italian biscotti and are perfect served with a pud or even dipped in sweet wine.

Makes 50

3 egg whites
85g caster sugar
¼ teaspoon ground cinnamon
grated zest of 1 orange
115g plain flour
115g mixed dried fruit, chopped

Preheat the oven to 160°C/gas mark 3.

Lightly oil the base and sides of a 25cm rectangular shallow cake tin. Line with baking parchment paper, bringing the paper up and over the sides.

Using an electric whisk, beat the eggs to soft peaks in a large bowl. With the whisk running, add the caster sugar in a steady stream until the egg whites are glossy. With a spoon, fold in the remaining ingredients.

Spoon the mixture into the cake tin and smooth over the top with a palette knife. Bake in the oven for 35 minutes until pale and golden. Allow to cool, then wrap in clingfilm and leave overnight.

Preheat the oven to 140°C/gas mark 1.

Turn the biscuit out onto your counter and cut across the short side in very thin slices. Break the slices into different sizes and place on a rack. Return to the oven and cook for 15–20 minutes until crisp. Allow to cool, then store in an airtight container for up to one week.

Per serving

118 cals　　　　0.9g fibre

1.7g fat　　　　0.9g salt

0.7g saturates

1.6g sugar　　　**3g fat per 100g**

Herby scones

Makes 8

225g self-raising flour
1 teaspoon powdered English mustard
½ teaspoon sweet paprika
½ teaspoon salt
1 hot red chilli, deseeded and diced
2 teaspoons snipped chives
1 teaspoon finely chopped thyme
100g low-fat soft cheese
½ teaspoon finely chopped rosemary
2 teaspoons Worcestershire sauce
100ml skimmed milk

Preheat the oven to 200°C/gas mark 6.

Sift the flour, mustard, paprika and salt into a bowl then add the chilli, chives, thyme, soft cheese and rosemary, mixing well to combine.

Make a well in the centre of the mixture, then add the Worcestershire sauce and gradually add the milk, mixing until you have a soft dough. (You should have a little milk left over for brushing the scone before baking.)

Turn out the dough onto a floured surface and gently knead to bring everything together. Roll out to about 2cm thickness then stamp out your scones using a 4–5cm plain pastry cutter ring. Collect up any dough trimmings, re-roll and stamp out a couple more.

Brush the scones with the excess milk and place on a flat baking tray. Place in the oven and cook for 15–18 minutes or until risen and golden. Transfer to a wire rack to cool. Serve warm.

Tropical fruit cake

Per serving
237 cals   1.5g fibre
1.1g fat   0.5g salt
0.3g saturates
36.5g sugar   **1.2g fat per 100g**

Having two Aussie boys, I've grown used to their passion for carrot cake and banana cake. Now I've created one with lower fat and a lighter flavour which I hope they and you will enjoy. You can vary the dried fruits to suit your tastes.

Serves 12

300g plain flour
½ teaspoon salt
2 teaspoons baking powder
175g soft light brown sugar
½ teaspoon grated ginger
1 free-range egg, beaten
pulp from 2 passion fruits
1 small ripe banana, mashed
135ml low-fat fromage frais
85g dried mango, finely diced
85g dried pineapple, finely chopped

ICING:

115g icing sugar, sifted
up to 2 teaspoons pineapple juice

Preheat the oven to 180°C/gas mark 4.

Lightly oil an 18cm round cake tin and line the bottom and sides with parchment paper.

Sift the flour, salt and baking powder into a large bowl then fold in the sugar and stir well to combine. Make a large well in the centre.

In a separate bowl, beat together the ginger, egg, passion fruit pulp, banana and fromage frais and pour into the well you've made in the flour. Using your hand, mix the wet and dry ingredients together, but without overworking it. Fold in the dried fruit.

Spoon the mixture into the cake tin and smooth the surface. Bake in the oven for about 50 minutes or until a skewer comes out clean. Allow to cool slightly then turn out onto a wire cooling tray.

Meanwhile, make the icing by mixing the icing sugar with the pineapple juice, adding a little at a time to make a soft but *not runny* icing. When the cake has cooled sufficiently, drizzle over the icing in a haphazard, streaky manner.

The cake will keep for four days if stored in a cake tin.

Roast Bramley apples with dried fruits

Bramleys are the perfect cooking apple because they become really fluffy and souffléd when cooked. With the sugars, orange juice and syrup I create a lovely toffee-ish sauce that will banish that yearning for cream or custard.

Serves 4

4 Bramley apples
25g dried blueberries
25g dried cherries
4 dried apricots
4 Medjool dates, stoned and
    chopped
25g porridge oats
½ teaspoon mixed spice
¼ teaspoon ground cinnamon
3 tablespoons soft dark brown
    muscovado sugar
5 tablespoons orange juice
1 tablespoon golden syrup

Preheat the oven to 200°C/gas mark 6.

Core the apples using a corer knife or melon baller; I find the latter works best as you want to get right inside the apple and hollow out more of a cavity to accommodate more fruit. Then, using the tip of a sharp knife, score the skin centrally around the circumference of each apple to prevent them from bursting during cooking.

Combine the fruits, oats, spices and brown sugar in a bowl, then spoon into the cavity of the apples. If there is too much, just scatter into the roasting tray.

Place the apples in the roasting tray then pour over the orange juice and golden syrup.

Cook for 45 minutes in the oven, basting every 10 minutes. Reduce the temperature to 180°C/gas mark 4 if the apples are browning too quickly or the liquid is burning.

Honey-grilled figs and friends

Figs are delicious but misunderstood – they live with the legacy that figs are good for producing bodily movements. Be that as it may, they are delicious in so many guises, both savoury and sweet.

Serves 4

4 figs, halved through the stalk
1 mango, peeled, stoned and cut into
    several chunky slivers
2 sweet oranges, segmented (the juice
    from squeezing the membranes saved)
4 tablespoons caster sugar
½ teaspoon ground cinnamon
90ml runny honey
1 tablespoon orange liqueur (optional)
55g pomegranate seeds

Arrange the figs, cut-side up, with the mango slivers and orange segments decoratively in a presentable baking dish. Combine the sugar and cinnamon and sprinkle over the fruit.

Place under the grill and cook until the sugar is melted and bubbling and the figs have browned.

Meanwhile, heat the retained orange juice and honey in a saucepan and bring to the boil. Reduce over medium heat until sticky then fold in the orange liqueur, if using.

Serve the fruits piping hot, drizzled with honey and scattered with pomegranate seeds.

Dried fruit and ginger pudding

Per serving

341 cals — 2.2g fibre
5.7g fat — 0.8g salt
2.1g saturates
44.8g sugar — **2.6g fat per 100g**

Steamed puddings are such a treat – they cost very little to make but they do require a little effort. The choice of fruits is very much down to you, the cook. Here I use dates, figs and apple.

Serves 8

85g dried figs, finely chopped
40g dried apple, chopped
40g undyed glacé cherries, chopped
40g preserved ginger in syrup,
  chopped
60g low-fat spread
115g soft dark brown sugar
60ml water
180ml skimmed milk
1 tablespoon malt vinegar
1½ teaspoons bicarbonate of soda
200g plain flour
½ teaspoon ground cinnamon
½ teaspoon ground ginger
1 teaspoon mixed spice
900ml low-fat custard

Lightly oil a 1.8-litre pudding basin and place a disc of baking parchment in the bottom.

Place the fruits and ginger in a saucepan with the low-fat spread, sugar and water and heat until the fat has melted, then cool.

Place the milk in a saucepan and bring to the boil. Add the vinegar and bicarbonate of soda and remove from the heat.

Sift the flour and spices into a bowl, mix to combine, then make a well in the centre. Combine the milk with the dried fruit mixture and stir into the flour. Mix well but don't overwork.

Pour the mixture into the pudding basin, cover with a disc of baking parchment, then cover with oiled foil and secure with string. Place the basin in a saucepan and pour enough boiling water around the basin to come three-quarters of the way up. Pop a lid on the pan and boil for 1½–1¾ hours or until firm. Top up the water level with boiling water as necessary.

Turn the pudding out onto a serving dish and serve with low-fat custard.

Malted tea bread with blackberry and apple spread

Per serving
352 cals
2.9g fat
0.1g saturates
48.2g sugar

6.9g fibre
0.6g salt

1.2g fat per 100g

I love these sorts of loaves, which bring back childhood memories of tea with Gran. I mixed my dried fruits but feel free to use the same quantities of whatever you have in your cupboard.

Serves 6–8

175g porridge oats
115g soft dark brown sugar
½ teaspoon ground cinnamon
½ teaspoon mixed spice
85g dried blueberries
85g dried cherries
140g dried apricots, chopped
300ml made-up and strained Earl Grey
   tea, cold
2 tablespoons malt extract
175g self-raising wholemeal flour
½ teaspoon salt
1½ teaspoons baking powder

FRUIT SPREAD:

275g blackberries
1 large Bramley apple, peeled, cored
   and chopped
300ml unsweetened apple juice

Preheat the oven to 180°C/gas mark 4 and lightly oil and line a 1kg loaf tin or terrine mould with greaseproof paper.

Place the porridge oats, sugar, cinnamon, mixed spice and dried fruits in a bowl with the tea and malt extract. Soak for 1 hour, stirring from time to time.

Sift in the flour, salt and baking powder, adding any roughage that won't pass through the sieve. Bring the mixture together but don't overwork.

Spoon into your lined tin, place in the oven and bake for 1½ hours, or until a skewer comes out clean. Leave to cool for 15 minutes then turn out onto a rack to cool completely.

Meanwhile, for the fruit spread, place all the ingredients in a saucepan and bring to the boil. Reduce the heat and simmer until thick and very little liquid remains – you'll have to stir regularly. Push the fruit mixture through a sieve to remove the seeds then allow to cool.

Serve slices of the bread with the spread.

Double rose and rosé jelly with fresh raspberries

Per serving
221 cals
0.2g fat
0.1g saturates
33.5g sugar

1.4g fibre
0g salt

0.1g fat per 100g

Pink is very much the colour of summer, so this refreshing pudding is perfect for outdoor dining, plus jelly is the ultimate fat-free pud! As the raspberries are not set into the jelly, you may prefer to substitute quartered strawberries or blueberries. For those not on a low-fat diet you may like to offer some Jersey cream...Oh dear, I'm such a tease!

Serves 6

750ml/1 bottle of your favourite rosé wine
150g caster sugar
240ml water
1 tablespoon rose water
2 tablespoons raspberry liqueur (optional)
8 leaves gelatine
325g fresh raspberries
a handful of unsprayed rose petals (optional)

Put the rosé wine, caster sugar and water into a saucepan, bring to the boil, reduce the heat and simmer for 5 minutes. (The sugar will dissolve before boiling but to get a really sparkling jelly, follow my instructions.) Remove from the heat and fold in the rose water and liqueur if using.

Meanwhile, soften your gelatine leaves in plenty of cold water until the leaves swell (bloom), then drain and squeeze out as much excess liquid as you can. Stir the gelatine into the hot rosé liquid, cover and place in the fridge to set.

Once the jelly has set completely, using a knife, chop the jelly in the bowl until you have a shimmering pile of jelly.

Alternatively, spoon the loose jelly and the raspberries into glasses and garnish with unsprayed rose petals.

Per serving
196 cals
3.5g fat
1g saturates
32.7g sugar

1.4g fibre
0.2g salt

2.7g fat per 100g

Passion fruit and mango soufflés

Everyone is scared of a soufflé, but it's truly just a case of following the basics. This soufflé is a very light offering, without a roux base, so eat it as soon as it comes out of the oven. It would go nicely with a dollop of passion fruit sorbet.

Serves 4

1 tablespoon caster sugar and extra for dusting
½ mango, peeled, cored and finely chopped
2 egg yolks
7 passion fruit, sieved to remove seeds
2 tablespoons vodka (optional)
85g icing sugar
4 egg whites (at room temperature)

Preheat the oven to 200°C/gas mark 6. Lightly grease four soufflé ramekins then dust with caster sugar and divide the mango between the dishes.

Whisk the egg yolks with the passion fruit purée, vodka (if using) and a third of the icing sugar until frothy and well combined.

Beat the egg whites at room temperature in a very clean bowl. When soft peaks are reached, gradually beat in the remaining icing sugar until the egg whites are glossy and stiff. Fold one spoonful of the egg white into the passion fruit to slacken the mixture, then carefully fold in the remainder.

Spoon the mixture into the soufflé dishes, then run your thumb around the rim to help an even rise. Bake in the oven for 12–14 minutes until golden and risen. Remove from the oven, dust with icing sugar and serve.

Baked summer fruit parcels

Per serving

179 cals	3.2g fibre
0.2g fat	0.1g salt
0g saturates	
27.2g sugar	**0.1g fat per 100g**

I love warm fruit, even in the height of summer. Heating fruit brings out its natural aromas and sweetness. Too often, many of our British shop-bought fruits are picked underripe and are pretty tasteless; this recipe addresses that problem and makes for a delicious pudding.

Serves 4

375ml orange Muscat dessert wine

2 tablespoons runny honey

1 bay leaf

grated zest and juice of 1 orange

1 vanilla pod, split and scraped to
remove seeds (don't discard!)

4 thick slices of orange, seeds,
peel and pith removed

115g raspberries

55g blueberries

1 peach, cut into 4 wedges,
stone removed

1 nectarine, cut into 4 wedges,
stone removed

55g blackcurrants, stems removed

4 dried apricots, diced

Preheat the oven to 180°C/gas mark 4.

Put the wine, honey, bay leaf, orange zest and juice and vanilla pod and seeds in a saucepan and heat until simmering, then turn off the heat and allow to infuse for 15 minutes.

Combine all the fruits in a bowl. Cut out four pieces of parchment paper, roughly 30 x 30cm. Wet one of the pieces and place in a small bowl, leaving enough overlapping to create a parcel.

Spoon a quarter of the fruit mixture into the parchment paper, making sure that some of each fruit is included. Cut the vanilla pod into four and place one piece in the parcel with the fruit. Pour in a quarter of the infused liquid. Gather in the overhanging parchment paper, creating a money purse, and tie tightly with string. Set aside and repeat with the other three parcels.

Arrange the parcels on a baking tray and cook for 15 minutes.

Serve the parcels hot so that your fellow diners can unwrap their own, releasing a beautiful perfume.

Tip

You can play around with the fruit. In autumn, orchard fruits would work well, but allow a slightly longer cooking time in order to soften the apples and pears. If serving this pudding to children, replace the wine with orange or apple juice.

Apricot meringue fool

Per serving
273 cals
0.6g fat
0g saturates
63.9g sugar

4.8g fibre
0.2g salt

0.5g fat per 100g

A classic British pudding which is based on Eton Mess but without the whipped cream. Preserved ginger adds a little unusual interest and the wheatgerm adds some extra fibre.

Serves 4

30g crystallised ginger in syrup, drained and finely chopped
225g dried apricots, finely diced
2 tablespoons wheatgerm
90ml water
2 egg whites, ideally pasteurised
3 tablespoons caster sugar
3 shop-bought meringues, crumbled
2 tablespoons loose-set apricot jam

Put the ginger, apricots and wheatgerm with the water in a small saucepan. Cook, covered, over a low heat for 5 minutes, stirring from time to time to make sure that nothing is sticking and the water hasn't evaporated. Remove from the heat and allow to cool completely.

Place the egg whites in a very clean bowl and beat to soft peaks using an electric whisk or a manual balloon whisk plus plenty of elbow grease. Add the sugar and continue to beat for about 2–3 minutes, until stiff and glossy.

Carefully fold the apricot mixture into the glossy egg whites, then fold in the broken meringues. Spoon into four chilled glasses then drizzle with a little apricot jam over each. Serve immediately.

Tip

If you haven't got loose-set apricot jam, you can simply heat thick-set jam to loosen it, or alternatively use a drizzle of runny honey.

Orange and lemon Eton mess

Per serving
180 cals
0.6g fat
0.2g saturates
27.4g sugar

1.1g fibre
0.1g salt

0.3g fat per 100g

Eton mess is one of the best-selling puddings in our restaurants, and in this low-fat version, I'm using 0% fat yogurt.

Serves 4

3 shop-bought meringue nests
2 tablespoons low-fat lemon curd
2 oranges, zest grated and then segmented
450ml 0% fat Greek yogurt
2 tablespoons Limoncello (lemon liqueur)

TO SERVE:
grated zest of 1 orange
sprig of mint

Crumble half the meringue nests into four glasses and drizzle with half the lemon curd, then add half the orange segments.

Combine the orange zest with the yogurt and lemon liqueur, then spoon half into the glasses. Repeat the layers, finishing with the yogurt.

Garnish with more grated orange zest and a mint sprig.

Index

Acknowledgements

I'd like to mention a few people who have helped me create this book:

To my wonderful wife, Jacinta and our two children, Toby and Billie, who continue to give me support and encouragement and without whom, life would be very different.

To Louise Townsend, my energetic and ultra-efficient PA who enthusiastically ploughed her way through my handwritten recipes.

To Fiona Lindsay, Mary, Alison and Mac at Limelight Management who keep me busy.

To my team at my pub The Greyhound in Oxfordshire who were on hand to stand in when deadlines loomed nearer and I had to depart from my usual place in the kitchens.

And to Judith Hannam, my excellent editor and her great team, including: designer Jacqui Caulton and home economist Aya Nishimura. Georgia Glynn Smith, the photographer of this book, also deserves a mention; a great creative talent who has a real eye for bringing food to life on the pages of this book. And not forgetting the significant contribution of nutritionist, Juliette Kellow, who analysed all my recipes and made suggestions where needed.

And finally to all of those out there who have been asking for this book – here it is! Whether your reason to pick up this book is for weight loss or specific advice from a health professional to eat less fat in your diet, I hope I've given you inspiration that all is not lost, apart from the fat . . .